A BRAND NEW BRIGHT TOMORROW...
A Hatter's Promotion Diary

Caroline Dunn

First published August 2002 by
The Book Castle
12 Church Street
Dunstable
Bedfordshire LU5 4RU

ISBN 1 903747 31 7

Typeset & Designed by Alan R. James

Printed by   Creative Print and Design Group
                Harmondsworth, Middlesex.

" I am pleased that Caroline has written about last season's success.

The vocal support and numbers of fans coming to matches was unbelievable and all the team and management appreciated this.

The amount of travelling last season took us all from one end of the country to the other and the support at some of the matches, Darlington, Carlisle, Hull, Plymouth, Exeter etc. to name but a few was quite remarkable.

Enjoy the book, written by a supporter for the supporters."

Steve Howard
2001/02 Division Three Golden Boot Winner

Eric Morecambe
_Luton Town's most famous celebrity fan, a line from
whose theme song inspired the title of this book._

ACKNOWLEDGEMENTS

Thanks to Mark Stephenson and Kevin Lowrie for being the other two-thirds of the London gang and making sure I get home OK after evening games - it's been a good season, hasn't it, boys? Thanks to Graham Brazier for being endlessly entertaining company on the interminable car journeys to away games. Thanks to Ade Macrow who, despite being a Tottenham fan, has adopted the mighty Hatters as his second team and has become a charter member of the Steve Howard fan club.

Thanks to Claire Davidge and Caren Clark for putting up with me droning on about football-related matters, understanding why it was so imperative that Howie should win the Golden Boot, and for voting in the PFA website Fans' Player of the Year Awards.

Thanks to Bontcho and Sylvia Guentchev for their fine hospitality; the staff at Balti Nights, Wellington Street, Luton for providing us with good food and sympathy after poor results; Wodney the Wobin, mascot of Cheltenham Town, for his "All right, darlin', did you have a good journey?" comment; and the Chief Executive of Halifax FC for doing his best to get the kick off delayed while we were stuck on the M1.

At LTFC, thanks to Geoff Stimson (website editor) and Cherry Newbery (club secretary). Thank you to Mick Harford and John Moore for being great players, great coaches and great subjects for interview. Also thank you to Joe Kinnear, and all the players who have played a part in this promotion season, but particularly those who agreed to doing question and answer sessions with me: Carl Griffiths,

Kevin Nicholls, Ian Hillier and Mark Ovendale - you were all a delight to talk to. Thanks especially to Steve Howard, who has repaid my faith in him a thousandfold (I told him in December I knew he'd come good, and I have the dictaphone tape to prove it!) and made this season particularly special.

Last but not least, thank you to my mum, my dad (especially for driving on those interminable car journeys to away games) and my co-conspirator and excellent keeper of secrets, my sister. This book is for you.

INTRODUCTION

There have been so many books written about football in the past decade, and I have identified with most of them. I read Fever Pitch when I was fourteen, and it made such an impression on me; it remains one of my favourite books.

But although I loved Nick Hornby's writing, there was an insurmountable obstacle preventing my total identification with him. The fact is - supporting Arsenal is nothing like supporting Luton. Some friends who support Premiership clubs have frequently expressed their amazement that I should sit right behind the goal at Kenilworth Road, and that I bother going to as many away games as I can, standing on a crumbling, open terrace for an hour and a half. I always give them the same answer - I can't understand why they would want to sit in the upper tier of the main stand at Highbury, or White Hart Lane, or Stamford Bridge, or wherever, and not bother to go to any other ground. Or indeed, sit at home and watch games on the television. Or even worse, just watch Teletext waiting for the results to come in. For me, half the fun of football is being able to shout at the players, or the manager, or the officials, and know that my words are being heard by the intended target. And especially at a club like Luton, where there aren't that many fans, you imagine that the players recognise the faces and voices of the regulars in the crowd. This is also why away games are such fun: the players appreciate our attendance even more and each of us individually is more important.

I have had a season ticket at Kenilworth Road since I was nine, and went to the occasional game before that. When I first started going to football regularly, we were in the old First Division (now the Premiership); now, barely thirteen years later, we are in the Third Division, the lowest echelon of English professional football. Our ground is a place with much history, but it's now a sad shambolic relic, with a capacity of less than 10,000. What makes it worse is that our arch enemies and local rivals Watford have carved out a comfortable niche for themselves in the mediocrity of mid-Division One respectability, along with their ground which even we have to admit is quite nice really, and their rock star ex-chairman, Elton John. This is neither the time nor the place to go into detail about why exactly our club has sunk so low, but suffice to say that it's mainly due to dwindling gates, poor teams and bad administration.

2000-2001 was the worst season I can remember. It started brightly, with former player and legend Ricky Hill returning as manager, under a new regime of directors, headed by multi millionaire and lifelong Luton fan, Mike Watson Challis. Sadly, Ricky was unable to produce the results we all expected, and left the club at Christmas. After a period when another former player, Lil Fuccillo, took charge of the team, Joe Kinnear arrived at the club in February. Despite everyone's best efforts, Kinnear couldn't prevent our relegation into the bottom division of English football - the first time Luton have been in Division Three (the old Division Four) for over thirty years.

If I think about our decline too much, I get very sad, so I'm not going to dwell on our downfall. Instead, this is intended as a catalogue of our first promotion season for twenty years. Apart from the fact that we have had some great results this season, it's also been memorable football-wise for me for other reasons. First, I have been running an internet mailing list for Luton fans since May 2000. It hasn't been without its difficulties, but it has been really rewarding, not least because I have made some really good friends through it (most of whom will get name checked throughout this chronicle). Second, and perhaps more excitingly for this football fan with ambitions to be a writer of some description, I have been writing features and interviews for the club's official website, meaning that I get to speak to various players and staff. This came about purely by accident; I emailed the Club Secretary, Cherry Newbery, with some suggestions about the club's PR and relationship with the fans, and she invited me to pop into the club to discuss matters. It ended up with me talking about my English degree and work for MATCH magazine, and giving her my contact details to pass onto the site's webmaster and editor. He confirmed that there was plenty of writing to be done on the website and was happy to take on a new writer.

Although this book is about football in general and Luton in particular, I hope it will be of interest to more than just Luton fans. I've often said that if I ever wrote a book that was autobiographical, it would be a cross between Fever Pitch and Bridget Jones' Diary. I don't think it's quite turned out that way, but if it's a tenth as good as either I shall be very happy, and I hope it is both amusing and interesting.

Non-league teams

It's summer, and I am stuck in an office for eight hours every day, Monday to Friday. Not through choice, but necessity - I need the money. I always feel embarrassed when I admit that I'm a student (which I am; I'm in my third year of studying English at King's College London), and I'm not sure why. Perhaps it's because a lot of students that I've met since moving to London are incredibly rich, lazy, and have little understanding of real life (for example, anything to do with politics, pop music, or sport). I wish to dissociate myself from this kind of individual here and now. I'm certainly not rich - if I was, I wouldn't be working in an office all summer in an effort to scrape together the money to pay my accommodation fees for next semester...and also to pay for my season ticket at Kenilworth Road. Luckily, one of the advantages of being a student is the discount on season tickets on production of an NUS card. So I am guaranteed entry to every single one of our 23 league games to be played at home this season, and I am looking forward to it already.

One of the most entertaining features of present day Luton Town is our manager, the eccentric, ebullient Joe Kinnear. A stocky but nippy left back in his playing days with Tottenham and Eire, he is now probably best known for his managerial successes at

4

Wimbledon, and more seriously his heart problems which led to him taking a break from football completely for a while. In 2000 he returned to the game, being appointed Director of Football at Oxford United, which he left after a few months claiming health reasons...and then promptly walked straight into the manager's job here at Luton. The Oxford fans aren't too keen on either him or us, now, for obvious reasons.

Big Fat Joe (as he is affectionately known) is always quick to tell us about all his influential friends in football who will give him decent players for a steal of a fee. He has promised to clear out all the dead wood that got us relegated last year, and build us an entirely new squad. Not only that, but he's brought back demi-god and Luton hero Mick Harford as his assistant. There is a feeling of quiet optimism around the club. This is why I thought it would be a good idea to go to our pre-season friendlies, first away to non-league St Albans, and then away to non-league Boreham Wood.

Now hear me out. I would not normally consider going to away pre-season friendlies, especially not against non league opposition, but St Albans and Boreham Wood are both quite close to Luton (a few stops on the Thameslink train) and I didn't have anything better to do. I tried to convince my dad that he wanted to go. My dad is a Luton fan of almost thirty years standing, and of course it was he who first took me to football. He was not keen, however, on wasting first a weekday evening and then a Saturday afternoon on the terraces watching a bunch of triallists and youth team players play against inadequate opposition.

So I went by myself. Strange as it may seem, I'm not the only one on the terraces. There are a good few dozen other Luton fans there, one of whom is my friend Mark, who has caught the train in from Hendon. I met him early in 2001, through the LTFC unofficial internet message board, when he posted a message asking if there were any other Hatters in North London. I was living in Wood Green at the time, so I replied, and we've kept in contact by email ever since. Prior to this pre-season, we've only actually met once, outside the New Den, purely by accident (I'm easily identifiable - not many girls go to away games at Millwall sporting an insane Anna Karenina style furry hat), but our correspondence is frequent and always about Luton matters. As such, he was one of the founding members of my mailing list.

We witness a fairly uninspiring game. The first team play the first half, and it is heartening to see new signing Carl Griffiths, formerly of Leyton Orient and Manchester City, form a decent strike partnership with Steve Howard. The reserve team take to the field after half time, and it is clear to see why we got relegated last season; very few of our second string look any better than our non-league opponents. Except, that is, for Stuart Douglas, a home-grown, small, pacy forward, who is always congratulated for his effort, but his striking prowess is often doubted. His play today both off and on the ball is amazing, and he looks a class above everyone else. Yet he still doesn't manage to score. This is the clearest illustration of why Joe is planning to bring in so many new players: it's no good doing all the hard things if you can't do the simple ones, like sticking the ball in the back of the net, well.

The highlight of the day is watching the pre-match warm up. Mick Harford, as coach, is in charge of this, and it is good to see the respect he inspires, and discipline he commands. Last season, it would be normal to see the squad split into factions, messing around and not warming up properly. You won't get any of that if Big Mick is in charge. Even the younger players are totally focused on what he is telling them. If we can transfer this dedication in warm ups to throughout each game, throughout the season, there's no way we won't go up.

No to Milton Keynes

The news today reports that Wimbledon FC are planning to relocate to Milton Keynes, a "new city" in Buckinghamshire, just a few miles down the road from us in Luton. When I say "Wimbledon FC", of course, I mean the chairman and directors. The fans are furious that the board are planning to move lock, stock and barrel sixty miles north of the area that gives the club its name. It's a pure business decision. Wimbledon have been ground sharing Selhurst Park with Crystal Palace for years, and Milton Keynes is the nearest large conurbation without a League football club. Logically, the huge population in and around the city represents a sizeable gap in the market, ripe for commercial exploitation and youth development.

This being the case, Milton Keynes is often vaunted as a site for a new Luton stadium. David Evans, Tory MP and our chairman in the 1980s, began to draw up plans for this move, but after huge protests by Luton's fans and the town's people, the decision was made to stay at Kenilworth Road (which Evans sold to the council) for the foreseeable future. Now, with a brand new stadium in Luton almost a reality after our chairman bought acres of land on the outskirts of the town, murmurs about relocating to Milton Keynes are almost unheard.

What would it mean to us should the Dons move to Milton Keynes? Would people choose to go and watch what is, at the

7

moment, higher division football, rather than come to Kenilworth Road? It's certainly a possibility; but equally no real Luton fan will switch their allegiance. We'll still have our hardcore support, whatever happens. It's also conceivable that even the die-hard Wimbledon fans might not choose to travel all that way to every home game, meaning no revenue for the club, and no atmosphere in the stadium, which would be off-putting for any potential spectators. I really don't think Wimbledon will ever move to Buckinghamshire, but if they do, then I don't think they will ever pose a threat to us. The one real difference they will make is that they will provide poor old Wycombe with some real local rivals: at the moment, they're having to make do with us and Watford (although of course despising the latter is entirely understandable).

Other news today: Mr Kinnear has instituted a new bonus system for the first team squad. Win bonuses will only be paid if we are in one of the automatic promotion spots (in Division Three, this is the top three). It's good to see that we're setting our standards high.

Home pre-season friendlies

It is a truth universally acknowledged that Luton fans will always find something to complain about, even when things are going well. I don't know if this is the same everywhere - maybe every club does have its share of whingers - but it does seem to me as if we're particularly afflicted with terminally unsatisfied people.

Tonight is our second real pre-season friendly, against First Division Norwich, and our team featured several new faces. Midfielder Kevin Nicholls was signed the day before yesterday from Wigan for a minimal fee; the Wigan fans have been flooding our internet message board to let us know how gutted they are to lose him, and to alert us to Nico's notorious two footed scissor tackle. Striker Carl Griffiths makes his third appearance in a Luton shirt. Former Luton trainee and utility man, Aaron Skelton, is back with us on a free from Colchester and has been appointed team captain. After suffering several serious injuries when he was with us before, he's carved out a decent career for himself in the lower divisions (although I am sceptical about his ability to stay injury-free for a whole season). The team also features several triallists, including former Arsenal man Steve Morrow and centre half Russ Perrett, playing for a contract.

We lose. A section of fans take this opportunity to complain about players' skill, their fitness, their attitude. Kevin Nicholls in particular comes in for some stick, looking as he does a little bit out

9

of place. This really baffles me. OK, it's never nice to lose, but surely it's better to lose in a pre-season friendly against a fair First Division side than to lose next weekend when the season proper kicks off? The whole point of pre-season friendlies is to re-accustom players to the pace of a competitive ninety minute match after their three month long break. They allow the manager to gauge the skill and fitness of both squad members and triallists. Tactics can be tried out and discarded if unsuccessful. So what's the problem? If a pre-season friendly is useful preparation for the important league season ahead, then as far as I'm concerned it doesn't matter if we win or not. If we were playing Watford, that would be a different matter, and I would heartily agree that a loss would be a disgrace. But we're not, and it appears that the fans' expectation level this season is exceptionally high. So Russ Perrett, the one triallist that Joe has decided to sign permanently - beware the dissatisfied Luton fan. The consensus is that we are too good for Division Three, and any dropped points this season will be a cause for concern. Woe betide Joe, Mick and the players should the team not happen to gel straight away.

Carlisle away

The first game of a brand new season is always special. This one is doubly special for me as I have my first feature to write for the club website. Geoff Stimson, the club's website editor, has asked me to write a piece about the journey, our longest of the season, and the game, our first in Division Three in thirty years. I've never written an article during a game before, so I'm a little unprepared. I pack my notebook and pen, anyway, and try to think about things objectively, as a neutral.

It can't be done. In the end, I write my article for Geoff as a travel diary, complete with times. This is the full, unexpurgated version.

6.30 Alarm goes off. After getting dressed, pack bag with CDs and books as entertainment for the long journey that lies ahead. I know I will neither listen to my CDs nor read my books, as I suffer from a total lack of concentration before games, but it's best to be prepared.

7.30 Begin drive to Milton Keynes station. Idly wonder how many Hatters caught the 7.00 train from MK Central. Every Luton fan I have spoken to seems to be intending to come, but I doubt that we'll take over a thousand.

8.15 Arrive at station. The place is packed with Luton fans, many taking up the Virgin Trains special offer of half price tickets, but several others paying full whack for a day return. The sun is shining, everyone is smiling, there's a general feeling of confidence and optimism in the air.

8.40 Platform for the 8.58 departure to Glasgow (third last stop being Carlisle) is announced. The hordes make their way to the platform, much to the utter bewilderment of the few people who are waiting for the train to Wales leaving 10 minutes before ours.

8.58 Train arrives, dead on time. Everyone piles on.

10.30 Make the error of purchasing food from the buffet car. Am charged £2 for a bit of bacon wrapped in raw pastry. It tastes of evil. Resolve to write a strongly worded letter to Mr Branson.

12.30 Arrival at Carlisle. The Luton fans descend en masse onto the station, singing, "Big Fat Joe's Barmy Army" and "We Are Luton Town". There's no threat or malice, just the continuing feeling of optimism and excitement. Most of us opt to go straight into the pub right by the station, where the hardy souls who got the early train have been since opening time, along with the several who chose to stay over Up North for the weekend.

As more Hatters join us, the mood improves even more, and an impromptu singsong begins - all the favourites are wheeled out (including the anti-Watford ones, and the return of that old standard, "One Micky Harford"), as well as the new additions for this season - "We Are Going Up". It's so exciting.

2.15 Set out for the ground. It's a short and simple walk, although lengthened by the necessary detour via the cash machines on the high street (my fault - too much money spent on food and drink, and I don't think to keep some money back to pay to get into the ground).

2.40 Arrive at ground. There must be nearly one and a half thousand Luton fans here. Amazing, bearing in mind the distance. Teams announced to an excellent reception. Bit of a surprise that last season's young wing back, Matty Taylor, is playing in midfield, and old warhorse Marvin Johnson is playing at left back, but otherwise team is as expected. Nerves and anticipation build.

3.00 Kick off! Finally this long awaited season is underway - the first step on our road to promotion.

3.25 Game is not going as planned. We're not stamping our authority on it, as we should. Frustration seems to be growing both in the crowd and on the pitch - Stevo Howard is subject to an extremely hard tackle and looks like he's about to lose his rag. Hope desperately that things will calm down, we'll get our game together, start passing the ball about more and get some goals.

3.28 Carlisle have a shot! It's pretty close too, ball flies over the top, skimming the netting.

3.46 Half time. We're disgruntled and disappointed at the somewhat lacklustre display against a quite poor team, but still singing, as we have been all through the half, safe in the knowledge that Joe and Big Mick will be thinking the same as us and will tell the team so during the interval.

4.03 Luton return to the pitch to another rousing reception.

4.04 Kick off. And straight away the ball is with young Lee Mansell (who is certainly in an offside position when he receives the ball, but wasn't when it was played), who crosses it in....and Paul Hughes, on his league debut for Luton, is in the back of the net along with the ball!!! We go wild, as do the team. Fantastic stuff.

4.14 Marv is subbed, Adam Locke is brought on. Taylor shifts back into defence.

4.15 Nicholls is brought down, and we're awarded another free kick, which again Taylor takes. Centre half Russ Perrett brilliantly heads it back across goal for Griff to knock in! 2-0, Griff looks as happy as we are.

4.32 Lee Mansell, who's been suffering with cramp on top of recovering from his injury, is taken off. Stuart Douglas comes on, to great acclaim.

4.32 and 5 seconds Stuart Douglas falls over, to even greater acclaim. Although many things at LTFC have changed over the summer, it's reassuring to know that some things never will. Bless him.

4.41 Carlisle begin to get reckless in their frustration. A high foot that catches Nicholls causes him to lose his temper, and for a minute it looks like there will be a mass brawl. Luckily the situation calms down quickly, and the ref books Nicholls as well as the Carlisle number 11.

4.47 Griff goes off to a standing ovation, to be replaced by Andrew Fotiadis.

4.53 We start to whistle for full time.

4.55 After booking Douggie for what we thought was an innocuous challenge (although it's possible that we could be biased), the ref blows for full time. We stand to cheer and applaud the team's much-improved second half performance, and especially the six debutants. The team, led by and encouraged by Marv, come right over to the front of our stand to reciprocate the appreciation.

5.20 Back in town centre, with an hour to kill before the train back down south. The pub we were in earlier isn't letting us back in, so a few of us decide to sit in the café just opposite. From our vantage point, we can see, quite disturbingly, lots of policemen in vans, accosting what do appear to be Luton fans. A few people were removed from the ground earlier, but it didn't seem to be too serious. Hope that whatever trouble is going on isn't as bad as it looks. Why do people always have to ruin otherwise brilliant days?

18.10 On the platform at the station. Much to our amusement, Watford Junction is one of the stops en route to London, so every time the tannoy man announces the said station, he is roundly booed.

18.18 Train arrives, on time again. I thought the train on the way up was full of Luton fans, but this really takes the biscuit - it seems like every carriage is populated by Hatters, with scarves and flags hanging in the windows. The songs continue, but this time we're singing, "Campione!" as well.

19.15 Everyone is on their mobile phones, trying to find out how Watford are doing in their televised game against Manchester City. One of the lads sitting near us has had a bet on us to beat Carlisle, Rangers to beat Dunfermline, and City to beat Watford, and stands to win a few hundred quid.

21.55 Back in Milton Keynes. A good few hundred alight here, and announce to a deserted station that it was "Two-nil to the Luton Town". The rest travel on to the terminus of London Euston for their connections to complete their long journey.

22.30 Home. However, the journey still isn't quite over for some other Hatters - at least two made the journey up from Hampshire, and they weren't expecting to get home until around 2am. They're anticipating the trip to Exeter with relish, as it is almost near for them, although it'll be another mammoth journey for the rest of us. Looking forward to it already.

Cheltenham home

This is one of the perks of being a writer for the official site - you get fascinating cryptic emails sent to you. Geoff mails me mid-afternoon on Friday to tell me that there will be a loan player in the side tomorrow, but it's a secret so Cheltenham can't be tipped off...

The loan player is Tottenham defender Ian Hillier, who turns up at 1.30 and is put straight in the side. It's a gorgeous bright day, and I meet up with some of the people from my mailing list for the first time before the game. It's a nice start to the season, made even better by the rousing reception given to returning hero Mick Harford as he walks out onto the pitch before kick off.

It's another unspectacular game, which we win, so who cares? Hughes and Griffiths get our two goals for the second week running. Cheltenham pull one back midway through the second half, but don't really threaten a winner. Kevin Nicholls is sent off near the end for a second bookable offence, but this is not to say we're a dirty or even a particularly physical team. We're certainly the superior footballing side and the end of the first home game of the season is marked with a vociferous standing ovation.

Les Sealey

On Monday 20th August, 2001, all Luton fans were shocked and saddened to hear of the sudden death of former favourite Les Sealey. Our goalkeeper throughout our glory years of the Eighties, Sealey suffered a heart attack. Famous for his temper (defences would cower in fear if they made an error), infallibility (he was loath to admit that he would ever have made a mistake) and being the drinking partner of Mick Harford, the East End lad frequently features as the choice for the Number 1 shirt in all-time best Luton teams. It's a little sad though that a man who made such a huge contribution to our years of top flight success missed out on the greatest day in our history - the 1988 Littlewoods Cup win - through injury. He moved on to Manchester United, where he was a member of the squad which won European and domestic cups.

Although of course our thoughts were with Sealey's friends and family, it was more than a little annoying that all the TV reports and obituaries referred to him as "the ex-Manchester United keeper". Les spent more seasons with us than them, and more than that he was our first choice keeper, not a reserve as he was at Old Trafford. Yet another example of the media's obsession with Manchester United. It's incredibly irritating. Still, all that seems a bit petty.

Today, partly due to the requests of scores of Luton fans, Reading agree to have a one minute's silence before our

Worthington Cup tie with them, which is impeccably observed, and for which we are very grateful. It's a shame our performance couldn't do justice to the memory of perfectionist Sealey. We lose 4-0, and we are lucky to get nil.

I am shocked, though, to come into work in the morning and read on the excellent Football365 website that an unofficial Coventry City page on Rivals.net has published a defamatory and inflammatory obituary of Les, who played for them in the early eighties. I follow the link to the Coventry site, and am disgusted to read the piece in full. Angry and really quite upset, I fire off an email to the administration of Rivals.net, requesting that the piece be removed immediately.

I am even more angry and upset when I receive the following reply:

"Dear Madam,

We are sorry that Luton fans are upset but the assessment of Sealey is taken from the Coventry standpoint. There is nothing in the article which is not fair comment. Apparently, Les Sealey is regularly voted the most unpopular Coventry City player of all time by Coventry City fans. Our publisher was at the League Cup semi-final against West Ham in 1981 - both legs - and left the home leg with the distinct impression that West Ham's first two goals were gifted to them by Les Sealey who was, of course, a West Ham fan. Obviously we do not intend any disrespect to Mr Sealey, his family, or Luton fans, but football is a game of strong opinions.

If you have any further queries or comments, please do not hesitate to contact us."

It's not often that I'm lost for words, especially when I'm angry, but this was a really amazing response from a supposedly reputable and respectable web publisher. After considering the issues carefully, I respond thus:

"Thank you for your prompt reply. I have to disagree. I think it is poor and lazy journalism to print such an article two days after the man died. It is not just Luton fans who are disgusted, it is also the wider media - see Football 365's MediaWatch column, which alerted me to the article in the first place. To be frank, I am outraged that a reputable and usually excellent web publisher would even consider printing such slanderous and disrespectful comments."

I decide to give Rivals.net twenty-four hours to remove the piece before taking any further action. The next day, despite their customer service rep assuring me that it was being "reviewed with a view to removing", the so-called obit is still up. So I email the fan sites of West Ham United and Manchester United, When Saturday Comes and Four Four Two editorial desks, as well as various national newspaper sports departments, and copy Rivals.net into the correspondence. The fellow fans agree to boycott their Rivals.net sites until the article is removed. Rivals.net remove the article. Ha ha.

Thinking about it afterwards, I don't imagine that Les, not renowned for his calmness or diplomacy, would have given a toss what Coventry fans thought of him, nor what Rivals.net thought of him, nor in fact what anyone thought of him. It seems fitting some-how that such a charismatic individual, beloved by the fans, should be causing controversy even in death. Rest in peace, Les, you'll be missed.

Karen's wedding

When my cousin Karen sent me an invitation to her wedding back in June, I am ashamed to say that my first thought was, "What about football?" Why would someone get married on a Saturday during the football season? Of course, in June, we were still waiting for the fixture list to come out, so I said to my mum that I would go to the ceremony if we had an away game at a ground that I'd already been to.

And so it proved. Bristol Rovers away, and I've been to the Memorial Ground before. My overriding memory of that game was that it was a dreadful pitch, and it was freezing cold. So I go to the wedding instead, having coerced Steve from my mailing list into sending me score updates by text message. My boyfriend, Nic, curse him, confiscates my mobile during the ceremony, telling me that I can have it back when the service is over.

If you look very closely in the wedding photos, you can see me clutching my phone behind my back, and looking vaguely annoyed. Yes, yes, we lost. Still, I think I manage to overcome my anger at losing to Rovers, a team who don't seem to have put together the form that most of us thought they'd show in this division, and I don't think I make it too obvious to the bride and groom that I'd seriously considered being elsewhere. When they read this, I'm sure they'll be very disappointed in me - I'm sorry, Karen and Paul, I hope you can forgive my selfishness.

21

Southend home

A very poor game. The difference between us playing badly this season and us playing badly last season is that now we have the ability to score goals. Having said that, it is disgraceful that we take so long to score against ten men; Southend have a player sent off only twenty minutes into the game, and then proceed to push forward, winning, and then luckily missing, a penalty on the half hour mark. This is just one of the chances they fail to convert, and we get two goals in the last ten minutes, one from Griff (again) and the second from the enigma that is Andrew Fotiadis.

The most significant thing about this day is that it is still summer. I love games when it's hot enough not to wear a coat. Today I'm sporting my replica shirt from last season and my cut off jeans, and it's still lovely and warm. We football fans must make the most of days like this, because all too soon we're in the depths of winter, wearing eight layers and are still unable to move our toes because of the cold.

September 1st, 2001

Exeter away, and Engerland

How stupid are people who go on holiday during the football season? Yes, you guessed it, my parents and my sister, Pip, are away in Spain this week, so I have the familial house to myself. On the Saturday, I have the choice between having a lie-in, then getting up, eating junk food and watching England play Germany on Sky Sports - or getting up really early, catching a bus to Luton, taking a train into London, changing at Paddington to go to Exeter by myself to watch the Town. No contest.

So up I get at 6.00. I'm in London by 9.30, and in Exeter around 1-ish. It's a beautiful sunny day, and very hot, and it's a bit of an effort to make the long walk from the station to the ground, especially with my abysmal sense of direction misleading me. Still, I make it there, and witness a dreadful performance.

Exeter are currently second bottom of Division Three, and are really not very good. Yet we cannot manage to beat them. We are playing with the vertically challenged front two of Stuart Douglas and Carl Griffiths, with the giant Steve Howard on the bench, so the rest of the team decide to lump forward high balls for them to chase. This tactic does not alter in the second half, when the equally short Liam George and the slightly taller and incredibly injury prone Andrew Fotiadis replace them. It's mind-numbing stuff.

We grind out a 2-2 draw, playing most of the second half with 10 men after Paul Hughes is dismissed for a wild two footed

23

challenge. Joe Kinnear seems to think after the game that Hughesie was unlucky, and certainly he would have had a better view of the tackle from the dugout than I did. However, from where I was standing it was a reckless lunge (I think the Exeter player's boot actually flew into the crowd) and such a classy and experienced pro as Paul Hughes really ought to have known better.

The highlight is Joe's post match comment on the referee's performance, which he describes as "minging". Minging? Joe appears to have been watching too many teenage soap operas and adopted their vernacular. Bless him.

So a long train journey home, while the Engerland game kicks off at 6. I am not entirely surprised to receive a phone call from Nic five minutes into the game, who tells me that Carsten Jancker has put Germany ahead. (Interesting aside: Jancker was once on trial at Luton, during David Pleat's second reign. He was rejected.) I am more surprised at the flurry of phone calls over the next hour and a half, as Engerland respond in style with five goals, three of which are a Michael Owen hat trick. I get back to Luton just before 10, and back home just after 11, in time to watch the complete re-run of the Engerland game on Sky Sports at midnight. Fantastic.

September 4th, 2001

Club Open Evening

Every so often, the club throws open its doors and invites fans to have a nose round the offices and changing rooms, with players and key staff on hand for a chat or to answer any questions. Usually this is held in the summer, but as last season was so dire, it was cancelled and rearranged for today, a Tuesday evening. Quite a few fans make the effort to travel into Luton, and we get the chance to wander round and mingle. Players on these occasions always seem a little bit uncomfortable; I'm guessing it's not because they're aloof or stand-offish, but rather because they're a bit embarrassed about the hero worship from grown-up people to which they're subject. Give them their due, though, they're all very good with the young fans; goalkeeper Mark Ovendale has his picture taken with a toddler, who he holds in his arms - inevitably some wag shouts out, "Don't give that baby to him! He'll drop it!"

Steve Howard is standing by himself looking a bit lost when I arrive, so I go over to him to say hello, and that I hope he'll be back in the team on Saturday, which he seems to appreciate. I'm clutching my dictaphone under orders to write a brief article about the evening, so I get a few soundbites from club secretary Cherry about how successful the event has been, before wandering across town to grab a curry and a few drinks before heading home.

My Grandma

All my grandparents live in St Albans, and both my parents were brought up there. Bearing in mind that St Albans is in Hertfordshire, I thank my lucky stars every day that my dad chose to follow the righteous path of supporting Luton, instead of straying over to the Dark Side of the evil that dwells just down the M1.

Over the past three years, though, my grandma has developed Alzheimer's disease, and as my grandad couldn't cope with her any more (he suffers from poor health himself) she now lives in a residential home not too far from my parents' house in Dunstable. This is good because it means one of us can go in to see her every day. Yet this in itself can sometimes be distressing - if she's in a particularly forgetful mood, for example, and can't remember our names, although she always recognises our faces.

This week, as my family are on holiday, it's my sole responsibility to look after her. Obviously I don't mind - as she can't deal with more than two visitors at once, it's usually my mum and my sister who go to see her if I'm not home from work and stuck in traffic (which is frequent). For some reason, she's always very co-operative with me and I find her quite easy to handle, even if she's in an argumentative mood. We have a few nice evenings together over the course of the week, and manage to have some quite lucid conversations.

I am very distressed then when I get a phone call on Thursday morning telling me that Grandma has been taken into hospital. I ring work and tell them I won't be in, and take a taxi up to A&E. After spending several hours there, she's diagnosed with internal bleeding of some description, possibly from a stomach ulcer due to the amounts of painkillers that she has been prescribed for osteoporosis. She's admitted, and scheduled for an endoscopy in the morning. I spend all day and all evening with her, going home to sleep but returning by 7.30 the next morning. I go into surgery with her and hold her hand and watch on the monitors while the operation is performed (a horrible experience, incidentally, one which I never wish to repeat, and one which I would not wish any-one else to have to go through).

It is today when it strikes me that I am now grown up. I am speaking to surgeons and consultants and ward sisters, I am giving information about her medical history, and I am the one that even-tually all the medical and nursing staff concede can handle my grandma best. (I told them that she wouldn't put up with them tak-ing her temperature by sticking a thermometer in her ear, but they wouldn't listen, and so really they deserved it when she pushed them away.) More than that, though, I have another human being dependent on me - my darling grandma, who used to read me sto-ries, who taught me to bake cakes, who showed me how to embroi-der, who first took me to the theatre, who made me dolls' clothes and cuddly toys (including my Steve Foster doll resplendent in old Luton kit). She used to look after me on a Saturday afternoon when I was tiny, when Dad went to football and Mum was at work. And now - she is lying in a hospital bed, frail and weak as a kitten, not understanding where she is. I am the only familiar face she sees. She needs me. I don't leave her bedside until my family get back in the country on Friday evening.

It also makes me realise how intrinsically kind some people are. Of course, there are the fantastic hospital staff, who save my grandma's life. (And Dr Elias, I'm sorry for laughing at the questions you were asking Grandma, it was just so funny when you asked, "Do you know where you are now?" and she glared at you and snapped as if you were a total imbecile, "Well, I'm here, of course!") But also there's my cousin Joanna, who gets a taxi over from deepest darkest Hertfordshire, to provide me with moral support and to keep me company all day on Thursday. And there's my friend Rob, to whom I haven't spoken in a few months (through nothing but sheer laziness on the part of both of us), but who drives to the hospital as soon as I ask, to take me to collect some of Grandma's belongings from her home, and won't hear of taking any petrol money from me.

I don't think it's often that you have friends and family like that, who can be depended on so totally in a crisis. I can be a little bit cynical about human nature, but sometimes my faith can be almost totally restored. So this is a thank you to Joanna and Rob - you're both brilliant and I don't know what I would have done without you.

When my family get to the hospital on Friday evening, I leave my mum and my sister with Grandma, and go for a walk around the grounds with my dad. He's very suntanned, wearing his new Luton home shirt, and tells me he saw Mike Watson-Challis (our millionaire chairman) at Malaga airport with David Pleat (former Luton boss, now director of football at Tottenham Hotspur). As he's relaying the anecdote, though, we see John Moore, now Luton's youth team coach, but formerly a fearsome centre half in our great team of the sixties, and later manager of our most successful league side ever. He looks over at us and smiles as if he thinks he should recognise us, but can't. We speculate on whom he is here visiting; certain members of our squad are so injury prone it wouldn't be surprising if the hospital eventually dedicated an entire ward to LTFC.

Oxford home

Division Three is dreadful. This game - a one-all draw - is abysmal and instantly forgettable. Two early goals is the sum of the goalmouth action, Nico's goal cancelling out Oxford's fourth minute opener. In fact, this game is significant only for the injuries our attackers picked up - Carl Griffiths has shin splints and is suffering, and pre-season signing from Norwich, Adrian Forbes, is taken off at half time; according to Joe he was "feeling his groin". Hurrah for football managers, masters of the double entendre.

Joe is apparently claiming he is about to sign striker Alex di Rocco from St Etienne; he reckons we are having him on trial for the rest of this week. Why is it then that he does not play di Rocco in our reserve game this week, St Etienne have denied an impending transfer on their website, and seem highly amused by the whole matter? I think Joe has a trick or two up his sleeve...

York away and Ian Hillier

There was talk that the entire League programme would be cancelled today as a mark of respect to the victims of the World Trade Centre attack. That does not transpire. However, all players are wearing black armbands, and there is a minute's silence before the game.

It's a strange atmosphere. As well as the obvious feeling that football isn't very important in the face of such loss of human life, there are rumblings of discontent among the fans. Big Geordie striker Steve Howard is the scapegoat. He has scored no goals yet this season, and a vocal section of supporters want him dropped forthwith.

I'm not part of this vocal section, because Howie is my favourite player. Honestly. Of course I understand the arguments about him not scoring enough goals, but I think he's a good work-horse (that's workhorse, and definitely not carthorse), taking much of the weight from his strike partner, Griff, allowing him to get in the box and score goals. He also has an ability to read the game, an amazing physical strength and definite commitment to the cause. By now, I'm used to defending my favourite players; my previous favourite was Tony Thorpe, whom I saw in the reserves just after we signed him as a teenager. Thorpey scored over 30 goals in 1996-1997, firing us into the Division Two play offs virtually single-handedly, and still got huge amounts of stick from a minority who thought he was lazy and a waste of space. So it's not exactly a surprise when a less prolific striker gets shedloads more abuse.

Today, the anti-Howard brigade are out in force and making themselves known. So when we get a penalty at the start of the second half, it is no surprise that Howie, desperate to score, steps up to take it. But he is a little bit too desperate, and the keeper saves his kick.

Then the afternoon takes a turn for the even worse. As the rain begins to pelt down on the open away terrace, the ref orders the penalty to be retaken. There ensues a scuffle between Aaron Skelton (team captain), Kevin "Psycho" Nicholls (acting captain in Skelts' all-too-frequent absences through injury) and Howard. The big man emerges with the ball, and places it on the spot. And misses again.

What follows is something I have never heard from a Luton crowd before. They boo Howie every time he gets the ball. The booing and catcalls have a detrimental effect on a desperate man who's just missed his easiest chance(s) of the season, and he starts running round like a headless chicken and kicking everything that moves. So he is substituted before he gets himself sent off. He tears off his shirt in disgust, including the black armband in remembrance of the New York victims, and storms straight off down the tunnel, pausing only to shout at Mick Harford (never a wise move).

The comments being made around the terrace start to make me very angry. I'm with my dad and his mate Graham (who has been a supporter even longer than my dad) and we get so cross that we stomp off in foul moods to stand in a cluster of three on the edge of the ground, away from the nucleus of Luton fans.

Poor Ian Hillier, coming into this cauldron of emotion. He's a right back, around my age (21-ish); he's the player we signed on loan from Spurs just before the Cheltenham game. After Howard is taken off, Hillier is brought on and forced to play up front - we have no other attacking options on the bench. And yet Hills scores the winner, a fantastic chip from the edge of the area of which any striker of any league would be proud. An amazing goal.

Obviously events after the game (which, incidentally, is extended by an insane "minimum of seven extra minutes injury time) are dominated by the penalty incident. Big Joe's post-match press conference is typical emotional Kinnear bluster - "disgraceful behaviour", "no player is bigger than the club", "disciplinary action", you know the kind of stuff. The mood in the car on the way back is sombre. It feels like we've lost. It feels like the whole world is against poor Steve Howard.

After a good night's sleep, I realise that Joe has just as much a temper on him as Howie does, and they will both have calmed down by Monday, and it'll all be forgotten. A lot of the other fans though don't seem to realise this. Many of them are calling for Howard to be sacked, and wish never to see him in a Luton shirt again. In one way, it's quite funny that they don't realise that it's actually their fault that Howie was so desperate to score and was so keyed up that he missed both pens; if they'd given him a chance and hadn't slagged him off every time he got the ball, he would have been more relaxed. Yet that's really no consolation for all the vitriolic abuse that's emanating from so many people. It's horrible.

September 18th, 2001

Moving back to London, going back to Luton; Lincoln home

It's nearly time to go back to university, and today is the day that I have to pick up my keys to my new room in the halls of residence. This year is the first year that I have lived south of the river - the halls are in Dulwich (near King's College Hospital, surprisingly enough) - and there is not a single tube station nearby. There is however a mainline station just down the road, where I can catch a train to Blackfriars and then change there for the fast train to Luton. See, I get all the important things in life sorted out.

Down the other side of the hill is Dulwich Hamlet's stadium. Hamlet are in the Ryman League Division One, and I have heard of them solely because Emeka Nwajiobi, a trainee pharmacist at the time, came to Luton from Dulwich in the mid-80s. I vow that I will venture down to watch a game there sometime soon.

In the meantime, I have a more important game to attend. A Howard-less Luton take on Lincoln at Kenilworth Road this evening. I know that we'll struggle without him, but a more dire game I could not have expected. Just as against Exeter, a short strike force is unable to provide the team with any kind of physical presence, and we draw 1-1 after Skelts' goal is cancelled out right at the death by an unlucky own goal from Australian Chris Coyne, making his debut after a protracted transfer negotiation with Dundee.

Big Mick and Jean Louis Valois

The day before this home game against Torquay, I have the honour of doing my first Question and Answer interview for the club website. For these Q&A pieces, people logging on to the site are invited to e-mail in their questions, and then they are forwarded on to me to ask the subject. And my subject is Mick Harford - ex of England, target man extraordinaire, notorious hard man and drinker, and now Joe Kinnear's assistant and first team coach.

Only if you're a Luton fan can you fully understand what this means to me. I went into the club for a meeting with Cherry in the summer, and as she came out to meet me in reception, Mick walked past, and I was awestruck. He went into his office, and I stood there mouthing to Cherry, "That's Mick Harford!" She laughed, and called, "Mick!" down the corridor. He walked back out into reception, and Cherry introduced us. Mick shook my hand, told me he's glad to meet me and wished me luck with my work. I immediately rang all the Luton fans I could think of (and some who weren't Luton fans but were impressed anyway) to tell them that I had shaken Mick Harford's hand.

It's fitting then that he is the first person I've been sent to interview. He obviously knows I'm a fan, and does his best to put me at my ease (he asks about my journey into Luton, my thoughts on the previous few games, and so on) but - he's Mick Harford. Even when he's being nice, he does still have an aura of intimidation.

Anyway, we plough through the questions I've been sent to ask, and when I switch off my dictaphone he inquires whether there's anything else I'd like to know. So I ask him about his working relationship with Steve Howard (who even before the events of last week has been known to have a bit of a temper on him), the players he's been watching recently, and about our new signing, a midfielder from Lille by the name of Jean Louis Valois. Mick laughs, and says, "The French lad? Yeah, he's all right."

Not expecting too much, then, I go to Kenilworth Road the next day to witness one of the most electrifying debuts from a Luton player in living memory. Every trick he does comes off, he's running at players, beating them, selling them dummies, nutmegging them... If the day wasn't special enough, Steve Howard is in the starting line-up, and is greeted by a chorus of boos, and of course, it's poetic justice that he gets his first of the season this afternoon (at which point, I am ashamed to say, I stand up and start shouting and swearing at those who had been booing him, much to the surprise and then amusement of everyone sitting around me). And there's a hat trick from Griff. JLV rounds it off himself with an exquisite chip from outside the area, making the final score 5-1 (Torquay's solitary strike comes courtesy of an incredible own goal, a flying header from Kevin Nicholls).

It's amazing. No one can quite believe it. Monsieur Valois is the talk of the town, and indeed the division. From Champions' League football with Lille to Kenilworth Road with just one move. What a coup from Joe.

Leyton Orient away

And we go top of the league. Over two thousand Luton fans make the short trip down the M1 to witness it. Orient clearly aren't prepared for this number of away fans, and quite a few miss the kick off because they're still queuing in order to get through one of the two open turnstiles. Still, a 3-1 away win is fantastic: Howie gets another goal, as does Valois, and Taylor gets his fourth of the season.

This match is important for two other reasons though. First, Griff limps off towards the end of the game. It transpires that he is suffering badly from shin splints, for which the only cure is rest.

Second, my dad makes his claim to fame when he heads the ball back from the terrace onto the pitch. He is roundly acclaimed by all the Hatters standing behind the goal. I bet they wouldn't have been so impressed if they'd received a phone call the next morning, greeted by a whining voice saying, "I think the ball hit my glasses when I headed it back, and now I've got a big cut down the side of my nose." I ask you.

Sad news though reaches us during the day - Marc North, squad member during the 1980s, has died in hospital after a long illness. Our sympathies are with his family.

Team Talk

With the recent explosion of both interest in football and the World Wide Web, it was inevitable that there would be a proliferation of websites dedicated to the Beautiful Game. One of the most notorious now is TeamTalk, which has a page for each league and Premiership club, providing daily news stories. Unfortunately, this noble aim is qualified somewhat by the fact that their pieces are infrequently based on truth, and are more often than not rumours lifted straight from fans' discussion forums.

The esteemed trouble makers, then, who constitute the majority of my mailing list (the Barmy Army) decide today to stage a wind-up, commencing by starting a rumour on the LTFC fans' message board. It will be judged a success when TeamTalk take the bait and put the piece up on their Luton home page.

After much debate, the boys decide to spread the gossip that Paul Gascoigne is on his way to Luton. Gazza is selected for various reasons - injury prone so perhaps on his way to winding down his career with a view to retiring, the Tottenham connection with Joe Kinnear, the more spurious Geordie connection with Mick Harford... Actually, when Kev posts the first message, it does sound quite plausible. If I didn't know it was total and utter lies, I'd be quite excited at the prospect of Mr Gascoigne alongside Nico in the midfield.

Between them, the boys think of about a dozen aliases, and post messages in support of the rumour. We falter slightly when someone declaring himself to be "Mick Harford's Mate" says he's rung Big Mick himself to ask if Gazza is really coming to Kenilworth Road, and Mick just laughed. It doesn't seem to have dispelled anyone else's illusions though, and the ruse continues.

Until late afternoon. Someone puts up the message that the Gazza rumour is a fiction woven by members of a fans' mailing list, and as it was "getting boring now" he felt he ought to ruin our game. Clearly this individual is an insider, who subscribes to our list, otherwise he wouldn't have been able to read the messages. After much abuse and vitriol has been directed at him, he breaks cover to apologise, and promptly leaves the list.

And what makes it worse is that TeamTalk didn't bite! Still, it's quite an entertaining way to spend an afternoon. I heartily recommend it to any fellow connivers who wish to make news purveyors look foolish.

Plymouth away

The second game I've missed this season. This time, I am playing Mary Magdalene (no smart ass comments, please) in a local musical in the evening, and there's no way I could make it back from Plymouth in time for curtain up at 7.30.

This means I have to suffer listening to Three Counties Radio. I am nostalgic for the old days on Chiltern Radio, when Brian Swain, esteemed local journalist and die hard Hatter, did the match reports, which were fantastically biased and just what Luton fans want to hear. I'm not sure if the commentators on 3CR are Luton fans, but somehow I suspect not - they get people's names wrong, they don't seem to understand a fan's point of view, and tend to get sidetracked and talk about irrelevancies, much to the frustration of this Lutonian exile listening to the radio in order to gain information on the game. Having said that, I know that those permanently exiled from Luton games really appreciate the commentary and informality of the 3CR presenters; maybe it's something you adapt to. For me, the highlight of this afternoon's programme is the interview with Howie, who gives his opinion on the magnificence of the injured Griff's recent performances, then qualifies it with a laugh and the comment, "But he's a lazy bugger!"

This match has been given an extra edge by the fact that Joe has been deliberately winding up Devon's local press. One of the gems from his pre-match press conference was his remark about Plymouth's Graham Coughlan, "Yeah, well, he's no international, is he?" You get the picture. Some less kind Hatters have picked up the ball and run with it; one who shall remain nameless (but suffice it to say he is on my mailing list) went through the entire Plymouth squad player by player on one of the message boards, and the entirety of his analysis was, "Who is he?" We think it's hysterical. Plymouth don't.

So Argyle get a bit of revenge on us today, beating us 2-1. The one bright spot for us is the debut of Griff's replacement, and Howie's new strike partner, little Dean Crowe, who scores, and seems a more than adequate understudy.

Carl Griffiths

Poor old Griff. In fine form, with sensational shooting boots on, he's now ruled out long-term from the side due to complicated shin splints. He was voted the Division Three Fans' Player of the Month for September, which he seemed pleased with, but as with all footballers there's never a proper consolation for not playing.

He is the first player that I've been asked to interview for the club website, and the first interview that I have to do over the phone. The only problem with this is that I own a very erratic mobile, with no hands free kit, which means that I can't tape what's being said. I'm going to have to write it down, clutching my pen in my right hand, the phone in my left hand and hope I don't drop everything.

I ring Griff just before nine, when he's on his way to training, and explain that I've got to write the interview down as we speak. He laughs, and throughout the interview is very patient during the long pauses that ensue as I scribble down his answers. I feel very silly, but Griff is really nice about it, and makes me feel less stupid when he prefaces all his answers with, "Well, Caroline mate"; if I was really annoying him, then he wouldn't be nice to me, would he? Such is the life of a trainee writer.

Darlington home

Our first home game since the thrashing of Torquay. Another five goals. What's that I hear? "Easy, easy..."

Not strictly true. We always try to make things difficult for ourselves, just to make a game of it, and we gift Darlo their two goals, falling behind to the first after twenty-five minutes, scoring two ourselves and then letting them equalise just after half-time. But hell, as long as we can score five every game there aren't many teams that will beat us: Spring gets one, as does Crowie; Nico takes an excellent penalty, Howie gets yet another, and Valois scores another beautiful and skilful goal.

Ironically, it's Howie who wins us the penalty. After the ref's awarded it, Howie is lying on his front facing the Kenny End, with clenched fist and mouthing, "Yessss!" to the crowd. Funny boy that he is, he pretends that he's going to take the pen, and encourages us to join in his little pantomime: he shouts, "Shall I take it? Shall I take it?" and everyone is crying, "No!" (apart from me), so he grins and runs away, leaving it to his captain. The team are flying high on confidence, and it's good to see.

There are two other penalties in this game, both missed: Darlo have one awarded by the linesman for pushing, which no one else in the ground seems to see, but Carl Emberson saves it at a stretch. A few minutes later, Valois runs past half a dozen defenders after picking the ball up in our half, makes it into the box,

43

shapes to shoot and is brought down. Our regular penalty taker, Nico, has already been subbed, but instead of letting Valois take the kick himself in recognition of his brilliant individual work, Matthew Spring steps up...he hits it too high and the keeper pushes it onto the bar and over the top.

It's a Friday night, and as we're playing the day before everyone else in the division, these three points take us back to the top of the league...

Scunthorpe away

I don't like Peter Beagrie. Former class Premiership player, famous for turning somersaults after scoring, he rips poor Emmy Boyce to shreds down the right hand side today. He's also a sneaky so-and-so, employing what we perceive to be gamesmanship every time he's tackled, winning dozens of free kicks with a knowing smirk on his face. Fortunately Scunthorpe's strikers are very poor and can't finish the chances Beagrie creates for them. Equally fortunately, we have young Ian Hillier on the bench, who replaces Boycie at half time and deals with Beagrie much more competently. We get two goals after half time - one for Adrian Forbes, and one for Russ Perrett. Easy away win, simple drive back down South (courtesy of my dad) and, after being displaced last Saturday, we're top of the league again.

Rochdale home

Terrible, terrible. Where has our midfield gone? I actually genuinely forgot that Matthew Spring was playing at one point today. A silly goal gifted to our opponents on thirty-nine minutes was the sole strike of the game. Poor Dean Crowe and Steve Howard - neither of them stopped running or giving their all, but just weren't given the service they have every right to expect. This was a crunch game and we should have won to prove that we are the best team in this dreadful division, and make it obvious that we are here only for a year. But we didn't.

Halifax away

The fixture list came out in June, and this fixture stood out as a ridiculous one. What kind of fool would send Luton to play Halifax on a Tuesday night? How do they think we're going to get there? Do they assume we'll all take the day off work in order to make it up the M1? What about those of us who don't drive? Did they bother checking the train times? Did they realise that the last train back to London from Halifax would leave well before the end of the game? You have to wonder about the intelligence of the people who are running our game.

I had almost resigned myself to missing this game, when I met Kev. Kev is a Luton fan living in Brixton (which is not too far from where I'm living at the moment), who joined my email list at the end of August. In mid-September, I enquired of Kev whether he could drive, to which he replied in the affirmative, although he didn't have a car. So I said, only half-seriously, that he ought to hire a car, and drive to Halifax, and I'd give him petrol money. I still can't believe that's exactly what he did. Hiring the car from a place near his office in Victoria, he picks me up from university at 3pm, meeting Mark, who works in Tottenham Court Road, along the way, and we bomb up the M1.

Unfortunately there is a huge accident, and hence miles of traffic. By 6.30 it is clear we'll never make it there in time, so we ring Halifax's switchboard to see whether they can delay the kick off. Credit to Halifax, they are very helpful and said they are doing their best for us. No credit to the muppet ref, who says that as both the teams are there it doesn't matter if the fans are. It is really beyond me the way officials are so dismissive of supporters. The game wouldn't exist if it wasn't for us.

Anyway, we get there about 20 minutes into the first half, and all we've missed is Halifax's goal after three minutes. Dean Crowe hit two in quick succession around the half hour mark, but at the beginning of the second half, we concede another, and things are looking grim. An inspired substitution of Adrian Forbes for Jean-Louis Valois turns the game, and we hit two in the last ten minutes. Final score 4-2 to us, and the journey is made well worth it.

The trip home is almost as nightmarish. The M1 Southbound is closed for improvements, so all the football traffic has to go through some ridiculous village with winding roads. I bet the residents of said village are really happy to have hundreds of cars thundering past their houses all night long. We make it back to London just before 3am, not bad considering we stop for food at a service station. So Kev, this is your moment of fame and glory - enjoy it. Thank you for your fantastic (although slightly too fast) driving, wouldn't have missed it for the world.

Being a true fan

I've been winding Kev up recently, as he's missing far too many games for my liking. I wouldn't mind if he had good reasons, but he usually doesn't - normally it's silly things like worrying that he'll be late for a party in the evening if he goes to football beforehand. I do tease him a lot, but actually I know that he's a real fan - in his words, his "blood is orange, white and blue."

So how can you define a true fan? Nick Hornby reckoned the truly committed, or as he put it "anal retentive", fan is the one who would use up a day's holiday to make a Wednesday night journey to Plymouth. Now, I would do that. When I was working before I decided to go to university, I took a day off to go on the supporters' bus to Maine Road, home of Manchester City, who were top of Division Two and in scintillating form, to watch a Luton team stricken by injury and with no forwards. We were two-nil down within ten minutes, and we were lucky that they seemed to ease off after that and didn't rip us to shreds.

However, I can fully understand people not wanting to make such long journeys and use up a day's holiday; my dad didn't go to that game, nor did Graham, and they are two of the longest serving fans I know. So it can't be solely on games attended. There are people who live abroad and get to Luton maybe once every five years if they're lucky - yet they are bona fide Hatters. It can't even be on ability to attend games - Kev could easily get to some of the games he misses if he tried hard enough. My friend JC, whom I met at that Man City game, is going abroad in January to travel for six months. He is leaving the country and missing the majority of what should be our first promotion season in two decades. He and I know full well that even when he is in India, his thoughts will be with the team. Yet he argues that you have to have a life outside football; the season can't dictate your life.

So how dedicated is too dedicated? Where do you draw the line between commitment and having a pathetic life? There is a handful of people who are renowned for attending every Luton game and being heavily involved in the supporters' club organisations; they are figures of fun for another, cruel but sizeable, section of fans. One teenage fan professes to have missed A level exams to go to a reserve game - that's just silly. I pride myself on not being like that.

Then I realise - I was considering not going to my cousin's wedding in favour of a football game. I've told one of my best mates, Gary, that I shall be late to his 21st birthday party in January as we have an evening fixture against Bristol Rovers. Nic sees me rarely these days as I'm going to every game. Basically, I am a not very nice human being, with no loyalty to the people who love me. And I would never have realised it if Kev hadn't pointed it out. Cheers, mate.

Swansea home

A good three-nil home win against a very poor Swansea side takes us back to the summit of Division Three. More significantly, we manage to keep a clean sheet, instead of gifting the opposition easy chances, or, even worse, own goals. Perrett and Coyne look an excellent pair of centre backs, and I just hope that they can stay injury free so that we can keep a settled defensive line-up. The full backs today are Aaron Skelton, deemed fit for a change, and right-footed Ian Hillier, doing an excellent job filling in at left back for the suspended Taylor.

Dean Crowe, fresh from signing a two year contract, gets the first goal but is subbed halfway through the first half after being clattered on his ankle. He's replaced by Adrian Forbes, an attacker in the Stuart Douglas mode, but with more goalscoring knack. Forbesy proceeds to run the inept Swansea defence ragged for the rest of the game. Perrett and Forbes both score to wrap up this comprehensive win.

The game is refereed by Paul Durkin, who has been criticised roundly and loudly for his performances in the Premiership. Refs are only human, though, and of course they'll occasionally make errors. Durkin, today, has an excellent game, using common sense and not having to brandish his yellow card in order to retain control. So, Mr Durkin, I am being utterly serious when I say congratulations on and thank you for an outstanding display. It's a shame that so many of the other officials in Division Three don't live up to your standards.

51

Dagenham reserves

Another Tuesday, another London gang night out. Luton have a meaningless LDV Vans Trophy fixture at non-league Dagenham and Redbridge. We know that our reserve side will be playing, we know it will be freezing cold, and on top of that we have to pay eight quid to stand on the open terrace of a Conference team. Despite that, Mark, Kev and I take the trip along the District Line to Dagenham East to see the has-beens and the never-will-bes that constitute our second string lose to a non-league team in extra time.

The night is memorable for one thing only, and that is the goal of Peter Thomson.

Thommo, a striker, was bought by former boss Ricky Hill for £100,000. He had played for Dutch side NAC Breda and non-league Lancaster City amongst others, and Ricky at the time declared that he "had potential". To us, even then, £100k sounded a lot of money to be paying for an unfinished article, but we trusted the judgement of our manager and hero. And indeed it seemed as if he was right - Thommo played one of his first games against Stoke and scored twice.

That was to be the sum total of Thommo's league goals for Luton. As I've said, Joe was not impressed with the squad he inherited, and bought new strikers who leapfrogged Thommo in the pecking order for first team shirts. Thomson was relegated to the reserves, where he has scored a fair number of goals, and he's been farmed out to various other clubs on trial, to no avail.

I have to say here that I think many Luton fans have been a bit harsh on Thomson, frequently denouncing him as useless and the root of all evil. OK, he's not a great player, and he certainly shouldn't be in our first team, but it's not his fault that Ricky paid so much money for him. As for his skill level, I've always said if I had to choose between a player who gives 100% effort but isn't particularly talented, and a talented player who can't be bothered, I'd go for the trier every time. At least you can coach a lesser player who wants to improve and will work for it. You can't make a gifted player try harder. Also, Thomson's goals for the reserves are often reported to have been ricochets off his shin, or a lucky strike, and so on. That demonstrates that Thommo does at least have a modicum of positional sense - he's in the right place to score goals, even if it doesn't always work out exactly as he'd like.

But I digress. I missed Thomson's debut in the first team in 2000, so at the beginning of this evening I am yet to see him score a goal in a Luton shirt. All my hopes are rewarded in the second half when he rises majestically and heads the ball straight down at the keeper's feet. Much to our amazement, the keeper stumbles, and the ball trickles through his legs over the goal line in slow motion. The few hundred Luton fans go wild, and after the celebrations are over I am forced to sit down to get my breath back as I have been laughing too much to remember to breathe.

Unfortunately, and against all poetic justice, Thommo's goal is not the decider. It's 2-2 after ninety minutes, so we move into golden goal extra time - an official version of the old playground rule "Next goal wins." Inevitably, Dagenham nick the winner. After the game, we are not too disappointed, as it's only a Mickey Mouse Cup, and obviously we have to concentrate on the league (although some rather scary people castigate us for expressing the view that this game is ultimately unimportant). And Thommo's goal was worth the admission fee on its own. Dagenham East station is closed due to a security alert, so we retire to the traditional East London boozer on the corner until closing time.

Kevin Nicholls

Today I have to do another of my Q&A interviews for the club website. I'm a bit apprehensive about this one, to be honest. Nico is a highly rated former England youth international, worshipped by the fans, and I'm extremely worried that he'll be arrogant and not want to talk to me, especially because I'm a girl.

I calm down a little bit when he leaves a message on my voicemail in order to confirm a time for the interview. He's obviously ringing from the club, because there's a lot of background noise, and the message runs as follows:

"Hello Caroline, this is Kevin Nicholls of Luton Town Football Club. Just ringing to confirm a time for the interview on Friday. Can you give me a call back? Um...when you ring me back, if you don't have my mobile number, please ring me at the club, because um...<starts to giggle> I don't know what my mobile number is...OK, bye! <general raucous laughter in the background, with various shouts of 'Yeah, good one, Kev'>"

I get to the club reception in plenty of time, and they've only just finished training. Nico comes out to meet me, trying to strap an ice bag to his knee while he's walking, and inevitably he drops it and smashes ice all over reception. He seems to be all fingers and thumbs, so I help him clear it up. It couldn't be, could it, that our hardman, our captain, christened Psycho by his adoring fans, is a bit nervous about being interviewed by me?

Luckily my own clumsiness comes to my rescue. I've been lugging my laptop computer around with me all day, and somehow I've managed to unclip the hook on the strap and can't get it back in place. Once Nico and I have sat down in the players' bar, I ask him if he could have a go at fixing it for me. He readily obliges, fixing it straightaway, and now seems more comfortable, and when we get into the swing of the interview he opens up a bit more. He has a big smile on his face when he is telling me about his baby girl and his girlfriend, and their plans to get a new house. He also tells me anecdotes from his past career that I would love to put on the site but can't. (And no, I can't put them in this book either.)

Although I have always admired Nico's commitment, I have not always been a great fan of the way he plays football - he has a tendency to pick up needless bookings, and I have not yet been convinced that he is captain material. But it's still early in the season, and I would be delighted if he proves me wrong. I must say, however, that he is one of the sweetest people I have ever had the pleasure to meet. Anyone less like his on-the-pitch persona it would be difficult to imagine.

Mansfield away; Chris Greenacre

Although I have utmost faith in Big Fat Joe, sometimes I do wish he'd keep his mouth shut. He has been very vocal in his desire to sign Mansfield striker Chris Greenacre, upsetting both the Stags' management and fans with his implications that any decent player would rather come to Luton, a club with prospects, than stay at small-time Mansfield. Mansfield's manager and chief executive have since categorically stated that they will not be selling Greenacre in the near term future, and if and when they do, it will not be to a club in the same division. Greenacre's agent is reportedly chasing wages of £6000 a week for his client anyway, which rules him out as a potential Hatter, because Joe has instituted a strict wage structure, with bonuses for good results and position in the table.

Yet some Luton fans refuse to give up on the possibility of signing Greenacre. "Why shouldn't he sign for us?" they plaintively wail. To which the rest of us reply, "Because Joe says he's not going to pay his wages and Mansfield said they're not going to sell him and certainly not to us?" One particular individual asked me why I was so against signing such a prolific striker, and did I not agree that he would guarantee us promotion.

I would have to say no, I don't agree that he would guarantee us promotion. Obviously I'm not opposed to signing players that would truly improve our squad, and Greenacre would undoubtedly be an asset (although at the moment I'm not sure where he'd fit in to our tactics, playing as we are a 4-4-2, with little Crowie feeding off Howie). I've had this discussion with my dad before, and we agreed that to say that one player, even one goalscorer, would assure us of our place in the top three is naive. Presumably these people would argue that a partnership of Crowe, a prolific striker himself and well on the way to getting twenty goals this season, and Greenacre, capable of getting at least thirty in this league, would bring us a minimum of fifty goals. This is an incredibly simplistic view. These fifty goals have still got to be created - you can't score goals if you're not making chances. If you extended the Crowe/Greenacre/fifty goals theory to its logical conclusion, then it would state that if you packed your team with ten excellent strikers, then you'd score over 200 goals a season and get promoted. Not going to happen.

Having said that, it might be worth breaking the bank to sign Greenacre just for a laugh, in order to scupper Mansfield's chances of promotion. With due respect to them, they do appear to be a one-man team (though well organised), based around the clinical finishing of Greenacre, and that's why they thrash us today. We never get going, and although we get a consolation goal there is no chance of us getting back into it. A dreadful day is topped off by Coyne's sending off towards the end, and subsequent scuffles between several players. It does appear that Mansfield fans are just as shocked as we are at such a comprehensive result, emphasised by the way the announcer proclaims the Man of the Match award - "Today's man of the match is - the whooooole teeeeeeeeam!"

Although I am still positive that we will get automatic promotion, it is a little worrying that we have not managed to beat any of our rivals for a top three place.

Shrewsbury home

It's been snowing in Luton today. Luckily it hasn't settled, and the game goes ahead. It's yet another Friday night game, so we can all watch the Engerland friendly on television tomorrow. We've slipped down to third place, and need the three points to ensure the gap between us and leaders Plymouth doesn't increase. We make hard work of the victory, Matthew Spring hitting the only goal of the game in the second half. In truth, it should have been more comfortable. Dean Crowe and Steve Howard both miss chances I'm sure they know they should really have put away. But a one nil win gets us the points we need, and means that our job is done.

Bontcho Guentchev

There are various career paths open to the ex professional footballer - coaching, management, TV punditry...or opening a country pub (popular with those retiring in the 1970s). Luton's former Bulgarian international, Bontcho Guentchev, decided on something totally different. With his wife, he opened a coffee bar in West Kensington, Striker, and tonight, Kev, Mark and I give him the honour of our custom.

Our plan for a night at Bontch's wasn't without its drawbacks. Mark rang the café to ask for directions, and discovered firstly that Bontcho wouldn't be there that evening as he is now playing for non-league Carshalton who have a fixture, and secondly that the place isn't licensed. Never ones to let minor inconveniences get in the way of a good night out, we meet up at 6pm on the Strand, and go directly to my student union bar. We leave at 8pm and catch the tube from Temple to West Kensington. On leaving the station, we appropriate an off licence and purchase two bottles of red wine, and make our way round the corner to Striker.

We look in the window, and we are stunned to see there, before our very eyes, Mr Bontcho Guentchev himself, resplendent in his Carshalton tracksuit. This creates great excitement for three Luton fans who have had a little bit to drink, and we go in and take our seats with huge smiles on our faces (and me nudging both the boys and going, "That's Bontcho Guentchev!" every three seconds).

After ordering our food, opening our wine, making cursory intro-
ductions and declaring that we are Luton fans, we have a good old
chat with the man himself, who informs us that he got injured in
the pre-match warm-up and so came back here to help out.

He seems quite excited that we're Luton fans, and in his limited English asks all about his old team mates and the coaching
staff. "Little Tony, the striker, he's very good player," he tells us,
talking about Tony Thorpe, striking prodigy, my favourite player of
recent years, now unfortunately with Bristol City. Bontcho is a little upset when, in response to his question about Stuart Douglas,
we tell him that Douggie is on loan at Oxford. "But why he not in
first team? And Andrew [Fotiadis]? Why he not playing?" This
provokes much laughter and a general rowdy answer of, "Cos he's
always bloody injured!" We laugh even more when Bontcho is
talking about former Luton keeper Tanny Abbey, now at
Chesterfield - "Tanny, the goalkeeper - he not very good, yeah?"
Bontch is equally amused when he discovers that Marvin Johnson,
the senior pro when he was at Kenilworth Road, is still part of the
playing squad at Luton.

I have with me a photo of me with Bontcho, taken in 1995 on
the day he signed, when I was doing work experience at the local
paper. I show him, and he seems really pleased, and asks my per-
mission to show it to his friend. Of course I agree, and Bontcho
wanders off with my photo in hand to talk in Bulgarian to his mate.
I wonder what he said. I hope it was something along the lines of,
"And this was the day I signed for Luton Town, the Pride of
Bedfordshire," and not, "Worst day of my life, signing for this rab-
ble, and they made me have my photo taken with mad teenage girls
who were totally starstruck."

Sometime after 9.30, Bontch puts the big screen TVs on, and
flicks up Teletext to check on the evening's final scores. We all
cheer when we see that Watford have lost to Burnley, and even fun-
nier than that they've only taken 131 fans up there. Then we watch
Champions' League highlights on Eurosport, and Bontcho tells us
exactly why Steve McManaman is such a good player.

A photo of me with Bontcho, taken in 1995 on the day he signed

When it gets to 11, we think it's probably about time we made a move, as the Guentchevs are no doubt tired of talking to us. They shake hands with the boys, kiss me, and we wave goodbye all the way down the road. A brilliant evening.

Luton reject, Luton reject

One of the best things about living in London is that there are loads of good gigs to go to. On the way back from Dagenham, we saw a big billboard poster advertising a forthcoming Eighties revival concert at Wembley Arena, featuring T'Pau, Go West, Heaven 17, Kim Wilde and, headlining the tour, Paul Young. The latter is probably the most famous product of Luton. Million-selling soul singer over the past twenty years, it's a little sad to see him reduced to playing cheesy nostalgia gigs. To be honest, we're much more interested in the rest of the line-up, and we book tickets.

The concert is a bit disappointing, to be honest. Go West perform quite a lengthy set, to my surprise, as I could only think of two of their hit singles. Inevitably they finish with We Close Our Eyes (as JC commented, with a wry nod to Go West's seemingly rather limited repertoire, the only single ever to have no B side). Heaven 17 manage to ruin their one good song (Temptation, as if you didn't already know), and the bloke out of Curiosity Killed the Cat delivers an extremely strange performance, avec hat, which he removes half way through his set, to reveal that he's now bald. How depressing. Second headliner, Kim Wilde, however, is fantastic, and manages to hype the whole crowd up. We're all eagerly anticipating Paul Young's arrival on stage. I start to shout, "We are the Luton boys, wo-oh, wo-oh", get some extremely puzzled looks, and decide to shut up.

The man himself takes the stage. And his voice has changed. Maybe he's just tired, or has a cold or something, but the mellow sound that everyone associates with him isn't there. As the set wears on without ever becoming interesting, my attention wanders, and soon it is clear that he won't pick it up and I might as well go home. So I do.

Imagine my surprise, then, when I go to my parents' the next weekend and pick up the local papers, and see that Paul Young was given the This Is Your Life treatment at the end of the concert. Yep, Michael Aspel walked on stage and presented the Luton lad with the big red book. And I missed it. There aren't too many Lutonians that are given such high recognition.

November 16th, 2001

John Moore

The next subject for interview is Luton legend John Moore. He's now our youth team coach, but has previously served as both player and manager, leading the team to our highest ever finish in the old Division One. He's held in great esteem by every Luton fan, and there have been an abundance of questions sent in for me to ask him.

He shares an office with Mick Harford, who is eavesdropping on much of the interview, and keeps making random comments. The funniest one comes during John's answer to a question about the comparative physicality of the modern game and the game thirty years ago when he was a player: "I always felt that no matter who I played against, they were always going for the ball." Mick looks up and interjects, "Except me." John roars with laughter, and says, "I never played against you! You were too good!"

Amongst other things, John gives his opinions on the current youth set up at the club as well as some forthright views on the proposed PFA strike, and as a result I spend one of the most interesting hours of my life listening to him speak. He's extremely eloquent and very involved; his love for the game and for Luton Town Football Club shines through every word. His knowledge is unsurpassable and his enthusiasm unrivalled. No wonder his youth teams have been so consistently successful: he commands great respect and insists on discipline and organisation from each of his players. I am proud to be a Luton fan when a man like John Moore is part of the club.

Southend away - FA Cup Round 1

A shambles. We have a good proportion of our team ruled out through suspension or injury, and our reserves are out on the pitch. It does not make pretty viewing.

With Howie suspended, Crowe and Forbes form a vertically challenged strike force, with no physical presence. Forbesy does well to jump to reach nearly every high ball played down the pitch towards him. It doesn't seem to occur to us to play ball to the feet of the little men. Maybe that would be too simple. We get two goals - the first looks vaguely offside, and the second is partly made by a sneaky handball from the Croatian Ahmet Brkovic, a former Orient team mate of Griff's, and signed last month on a free transfer. But with the ageing, unfit Skelton and the excellent attacker but weak defender Matty Taylor as full backs, we are roasted down the flanks, and Southend also get two. Surprisingly, we manage to keep ourselves on level terms until the final minute.

I didn't really expect us to win this one. Still, there is a bit of consolation; at least I don't have to trek down to Kenilworth Road midweek for a replay, and at least our promotion push won't be disrupted through fixture congestion. But last minute defeats are always galling.

Hull home

Dismal, dismal, dismal. Hull beat us 1-0. It's even more angering that Rob Matthews scores the goal. He used to be on our books at the start of the 1990s, and moved on to Notts County, where he scored the goals against us that sent us down to what's now the First Division. Tonight, we never look like scoring; all our best moves are flagged offside or stopped by Hull's good defensive work. How can we appear to be world-beaters one week, then fail to string two passes together the next?

To drown our sorrows, Kev, Mark and I go for a curry in Balti Nights, my favourite Indian restaurant, after the game. We stuff our faces full and drink a few glasses of wine, but conversation is minimal - we're not in the mood for chit-chat. We get to the station, only just making it there in time for the last train back to London. This is all right for Mark as he lives in Hendon, but not so good for Kev and me because that means we have missed the last connecting trains from the centre of town to our respective parts of South London. In the end, we get out at Blackfriars, and take a night bus to the Strand, where we can catch another bus to Camberwell (for me) then on to Brixton (for Kev). Except of course all the buses are running late, so we have to stand around freezing our arses off for the best part of an hour. This is truly one of the worst evenings ever.

Macclesfield away

This was my first game in over two and a half years as a single girl. Although my boyfriend and I had been somewhat unhappy for a while, it still comes as a shock to the system when you finally get up the courage to end a reasonably long relationship, even one which was making you both miserable, and even when you know it will be for the best for both of you.

My boyfriend lives in Ipswich, about 60 or so miles away from London. This may make you think worse of me, but I had not been to see him at all this season, instead preferring to go to football. As he works every other weekend, it was practically impossible for him to come to see me. I realised just how silly it was continuing this relationship when Kev pointed out to me that he manages to see his girlfriend (who lives in Leeds) about twice a month. His exact words are ingrained on my memory: "You have to make sacrifices."

So is it impossible, then, to go to football every week and have a successful relationship? Surely not. I suppose the obvious answer would be to go out with someone who supports the same team, but that would have its own set of problems. What about when your team loses? Imagine the atmosphere in your house on a Saturday night. And what if you disagree about the merits of certain players? If Nic was a Luton fan and was one of those extolling the virtues of signing Chris Greenacre, I would have finished with him long before now.

Maybe it's different for men. I would think that in general it's probably easier for men to convert their girlfriend into supporting their team and sharing their views on the game. Then the happy couple can go to football together every week, thinking the same things and having a lovely life, without having to make "sacrifices". But what if you both already support teams? I've read before about couples who support local rivals - I remember reading in a local paper about the wedding of an Ipswich supporting bride and a groom who was a Norwich fan. I really can't understand that. Surely they'd spend all day arguing? Or singing abusive songs at each other? Or setting fire to each other's replica shirts?

With all these thoughts swirling round my head, it's appropriate that the chaos was reflected on the pitch. A dreadful, dreadful performance from the team second in the table led to a 4-1 defeat. And by Macclesfield! Fourth from bottom! Some fans' displeasure is taken to an extreme, shouting abuse and booing individuals at the end. I can understand this to an extent, although I can't say I condone it or would join in myself, because we've witnessed such a spineless performance. However, it makes no sense to have a go at the players who have actually tried their hardest. Steve Howard is, of course, one of the players picked on like this, despite him scoring our goal today. He gets lots of stick towards the end, and he's not helped by the fact that his team mates are making him look stupid. Example: Howie is on the right wing, and puts in a ball to Adrian Forbes. Instead of waiting for Howie to get in the middle, Forbesy puts it in the box immediately - and the ball is promptly cleared. As the final whistle blows, and the shouts of disappointment increase, I call over to Howie, who runs across and shakes my hand. I tell him that he's had a good game and not to let the idiots grind him down. It's a strange thing, though; all these boo-boys who reckon they're so big and tough go silent as soon as Howie is within ten feet of them. Not so brave when you're confronted with over six foot of angry striker, are you, lads? The other player singled out for criticism is, amazingly, Kevin Nicholls - the fans' darling just a few short weeks ago. This is also ridiculous; the poor lad has taken a hell of a battering today, and when he comes over to applaud us for making the journey and staying till the bitter end, he does not deserve the comments thrown at him. He has literally bled for the Luton Town cause, and he is visibly upset by the way that his efforts have not been appreciated by some of the crowd. He stays at the front of the terrace for a good few minutes, answering questions and apologising for the team's poor display, and probably wouldn't have left if his team mates hadn't come over and led him away.

I have to say, though, if anyone had to beat us by such a margin, I am quite glad it was Macclesfield. It's their manager's first game in charge today, and he is David Moss, former skilful left winger and Luton legend. Geoff rings me on the way home, to tell me that he's got me Mossy's autograph. I thank him, and suggest that he interview Kevin Nicholls in the morning, as I suspect that he will be very grateful for the opportunity to voice his thoughts. Geoff agrees, and informs me that Joe Kinnear went ballistic at his players and has stopped all days off in order to bring the squad in for extra training. Damn good job. I have utmost faith in Joe's ability to turn the squad's form around. It's a shame he can't sort my life out as well.

Mobile phones

My next assignment for the website is to interview Ian Hillier, who it's looking like we'll be signing permanently very shortly. I leave several messages on his mobile phone's voicemail, but he doesn't return my calls. I'm beginning to feel quite hurt, when my phone rings, displaying a number I don't recognise.

Me: <suspiciously> Hello?

Male voice, strongly Welsh accented, sounding a little nervous: Caroline? It's Ian. Ian Hillier.

Hills apologises for having missed my calls and explains that his mobile was broken and has been in the shop for repair - could I possibly ring him and do the interview the following evening? We make the necessary arrangements. I'm quite surprised, actually, that he's rung me. I've learnt so far this season that, although all of them are nice people and pretty talkative in an interview, foot-ballers aren't the most comfortable of phone conversationalists. Indeed, a frightening number of them don't know what their phone numbers are. However, I suppose they would argue, in the words of Phoebe from Friends, "I never call me!" That being the case, my latest tactic for arranging interviews has been to send them text messages: that way they can deal with organising times and dates and places at their leisure, and they don't have to talk to me if they don't want to. It's working pretty well at the moment. I love my job.

Game postponed

I get a phone call from Geoff on Friday morning, warning me that it was more than likely that the next day's game against Kidderminster Harriers would be called off. Hit hard by injuries and flu, Joe was unable to pull together a team to field. Considering the size of our squad, that's a pretty big crisis - over two dozen professionals unavailable for selection, and a good proportion of our youth team out as well.

Arranging to postpone a game for these reasons is a tricky business. Notoriously, Middlesborough failed to turn up for a game once and were docked points, resulting in their relegation at the end of the season. This is an entirely different kettle of fish, though: Boro could have fielded a team, but it probably wouldn't have been very good, so they didn't turn up. We literally don't have eleven fit players.

Kidderminster captain Ian Clarkson mouths off to his local papers about how Luton are a big club and, instead of postponing the game, ought to play their first year scholars, as they are a part of Luton Town Football Club as well. He and his manager, Jan Molby, both accuse us of being "running scared". Joe responds to these ridiculous allegations in true Kinnear style: "Clarkson? I remember watching him, if he could run any faster he'd be going in reverse." He also comes out with the classic, "You reckon we should play our schoolboys? Yeah, you'd love that, wouldn't you,

71

because that's the only chance you've got of beating us." He tells them that we ain't scared, and we will whup them when we have our team back.

Any team which postpones a game have to report to a League committee to explain their reasons for doing so. Joe and club secretary Cherry Newbery give our account, and the League understand that we had no other option. They then take £10k off us, and order us to pay Kidderminster's expenses accrued for the food and drink they bought that went to waste. Another example of our national game's fine administration.

Hartlepool away

It's a long way to Hartlepool. More importantly, it's an expensive way to Hartlepool, if you're a student, can't drive, your dad literally laughs in your face when you suggest that he might like to go and give you a lift, and the train is beginning to seem like the only available option. I am rescued by Geoff, who offers me a lift in his ever-so-flash car, if I could get to Woodford tube station, which is in Zone 4 on the Central Line, for 7am. So my day begins at 4.30am, as I have to catch a bus from Camberwell Green to Liverpool Street just after half past five. Despite the London Underground's best efforts to delay me, I get to deepest darkest Essex at 7, and the journey (which Geoff estimated would take five hours) begins.

Five hours my arse. Thanks to my fantastic navigational skills ("Follow the signs for 'The North'"), and no thanks to Geoff's execution of an illegal and highly dangerous U-turn, despite the presence of a NO U-TURN sign (which he claims not to see), we are in a freezing cold Hartlepool by 11, and knocking on the door of the nearest pub.

It's an interesting team line-up today. Ricky Hill's most expensive signing, £425,000 keeper Mark Ovendale, is preferred in goal to a fit Carl Emberson, and Ian Hillier takes the left back spot, with Taylor moving into midfield. This display is a damn sight better than Macc, not that it could be worse; a more solid defence, a more penetrating midfield, and altogether a reasonable performance. Not only that, it is good because all the whinging muppets who sit there and complain and slag everyone off for nine- ty minutes haven't made this extensive journey. There's about four hundred of us there, and the majority seem quite normal.

We notch two goals in the first 45 minutes. From where I was sitting, I wouldn't have been surprised to see the first one disal- lowed for a possible foul by Howie on the keeper; I will be inter- ested to see it on TV tomorrow night. The second one looks as though Taylor hit it straight at the keeper, and I have no idea how it actually manages to go in. Still, never mind, they all count, and we go in 2-0 up at half time.

Unfortunately, the ref, a Mr Leake, is very bad. Quelle sur- prise. He keeps booking our players for the pettiest of offences. Now, you would imagine that the players might think, "Hang on a minute, he's booking us for hard but fair challenges, maybe I should be a little bit careful." And indeed that is what Joe says in the dressing room at half time; apparently he goes round to each of them saying, "Don't do anything rash, because you'll get sent off."

Enter Mr Hillier. Now I like Ian Hillier, but I do think he should have had a little more sense and tackled a little more care- fully. Anyway, as soon as he puts the challenge in, it is obvious to everyone that he is going to get sent off (he starts trudging off even before the red card is brandished), and my biggest fear is realised as Matty Taylor moves to left back. Aaaaaaaargh. I know what is coming and of course it does - Taylor panics, falls over, Pool score. 2-1.

Hartlepool are unlucky not to be level by this point anyway, they've already had at least four clear-cut penalty appeals turned down (including what seems to be a rather subtle handball from Howie). Now they are running rampant. But Ovendale looks to have recovered some sort of good form, and is making fantastic saves from everything that is shot at him. Crowe is subbed, having run his legs into the ground, Forbes comes on to play down the right, Brkovic switches to the left providing defensive cover for Taylor, and things look a little brighter.

I can only think of one other shot we had on target apart from the goals, and that comes from Steve Howard, who should maybe have done a little better. He is up front, in the box, by himself, with two defenders in front of him, and Spring making a run from behind him. Now I will (obviously) give Howie the benefit of the doubt here, because I don't think he saw Spring as he was on his blind side, and Spring certainly didn't call for it. Anyway, the best chance for a goal would have been if Howie squared it to Spring, but he doesn't, and a rather weak shot is saved by the keeper. After an insane four minutes of added time (why?), the ref blows, we all cheer, and Nico, bless him, drags all the players over to clap us.

Although not the most outstanding of performances, this result really pleases me because we've worked our guts out to hang on to the points. It's the kind of game that we would have thrown away last year.

Rushden and Diamonds home; Danny and Elsie

When I first started going to football, there were a couple who sat near to us, who travelled all the way down from Blackpool for every home game, and pretty much all the away ones as well. Through my email list, I've got to know Danny and Elsie Clubb, and today I interview them for a feature on the website, prior to our single goal victory over Rushden & Diamonds.

I am quite honoured, actually, to be allowed an audience with this eccentric, though undoubtedly lovely, pair. They have turned down requests for interviews from local radio, newspapers and even the club's own matchday magazine, edited by the greatly esteemed, and long term Luton fan, Brian Swain. I am the first one they've agreed to speak to because a) I'm only a trainee journalist, and b) I'm "little Caroline" who used to sit near them, except grown up now.

They estimate that in the past fourteen years since moving Up North they have travelled around 364,000 miles, averaging out at about 23,500 miles a season. Not only that, but they've spent in the region of £150,000 supporting the Town, including petrol, tickets and player sponsorship. Every home game, they get up before six on a Saturday morning, leaving the house at half past nine, and arriving in the Century Club, the exclusive supporters' club which requires you to stump up a great deal of money up front, some time after one. Today, Danny was up even earlier. "I was up at five," Danny tells me, "I had to let Mansell out - that's one of our dogs, named after Lee Mansell, of course. And then I had to let Kenilworth and Jimmy Ryan in, because they'd been left out all night - they're our cats."

Before meeting Danny, Elsie wasn't a Luton fan - "I was living in the States, and I hadn't even heard of Luton. But now, for that kind of money, you both have to be fanatical!" she laughs. Her first game was at Everton's Goodison Park in the Simod Cup run of 1987-88, when the Town won 2-1 in front of a travelling audience of only 51.

They have been members of the Century Club for two years now, which according to Danny was an effort to make Elsie's behaviour "more ladylike" at football by making her sit near the chairman and directors. Their sponsorship of staff began in the early 1990s, when they decided to sponsor Paul McLaren, now at Sheffield Wednesday, and first team coach Wayne Turner, presently the manager of Stevenage Borough.

So why would such avid Luton fans move so far away from their spiritual home? The answer is simple, and maybe a little surprising - a TV programme. " 'Wish You Were Here.' They had a quarter of an hour long feature on Blackpool, so we just thought, 'We'll go and buy a guest house up in Blackpool'. That was on New Year's Day, and by February it was all signed, sealed and delivered."

They married in the same year as they bought the guest house. "We got married on November the 18th, which was a Friday, then came down for the game against West Ham, which we won four-nil. Then we went on our honeymoon - a little tour of the south east coast, because we had an away game at Norwich sandwiched between two home games."

Travelling so far, it's a little surprising that they've only had one really nightmarish journey where delays on the roads meant that they missed half the match. "The worst game we've travelled to was Gillingham a couple of years ago. We started off at about half seven in the morning, because we knew it would be a horrendous journey. It was shocking weather - rain, wind, spray from lorries obscuring your vision on the road - and we had to drive at twenty miles an hour. Then there were traffic jams and roadworks, a few accidents, and then the police stopped me on the M6 for not wearing a seatbelt!" recalls Danny. "We finally got to Gillingham at half time, and at first they weren't going to let us in. Eventually they let us in through a side gate for a fiver. The only consolation was that it was all open terracing there then, and everyone else was soaked through while we were dry!"

The only other occasion when they've missed a significant proportion of the game was at Leicester. "We were in a pub before the game, and one of our friends assured us he knew the way to the ground. We ended up running around the town, climbing over walls, through allotments here, there and everywhere on a wild goose chase! We got into the ground about ten minutes or so after kick off." There's also been a few abortive journeys: "Three or four weeks running, a few years back, we got as far as Birmingham and then had to turn back because the game was postponed."

This season, with so many of our away games in the North, it's a lot easier for Danny and Elsie to get there in time for kick off. "Carlisle was an easy run, York was easy. I got totally depressed when Blackpool got promoted - I enjoy my Blackpool away games, it's always one of the best games of the season," says Danny. They're both close to membership of the 92 Club as well; they have only Rochdale, Kidderminster and Rushden & Diamonds left to visit, which, all being well, they'll have completed by March. And what do they do during the close season? "We get in the car, and drive down to the new grounds for next season," they admit. "It's something to do when you're bored on a Saturday afternoon when there isn't any football."

Would one go to the games without the other? "Not if one of us is ill. That's not fair on the other one," replies Danny. Then I point out to him that he wouldn't be able to go without Elsie this season, as he is banned from driving for speeding. He laughs, "That's what she says! 'Who's the one with the driving licence?'" They estimate that normally they miss only two or three games a season, but they missed a few at the start of this campaign as they had a holiday to Canada. They enjoyed their sojourn across the Atlantic so much that they're returning in the New Year for ten days, flying back to England for the Rochdale away game - and then going back out to Canada.

In their years of following Luton, there have been lots of good moments, but Elsie chooses the Littlewoods Cup win of 1988 as her highlight, naming Brian Stein, Ricky Hill and Mick Harford as her top players of that time. More recently, she chooses Julian James, Kingsley Black and Paul McLaren as her favourites. Danny goes a little bit further back and recalls the consecutive promotion seasons of the late sixties. "When you watch your team win a league championship, it's more special than watching them win a one-off cup competition," he says. His favourite players are mainly from that era - "Malcolm McDonald, Bruce Rioch, Alan Slough, Mike Harrison, Brian Lewis - I thought he was one hell of a little player." Inevitably he also admires the players of our great Eighties' teams - "Lil Fuccillo, Ricky Hill, Mick Harford, Steve Foster, Kirk Stephens, Les Sealey.

Both are optimistic about this season and the future. Danny sums it up when he says, "I think we've actually got a board in now who are Luton through and through and care about the club. And I still think we'll win the league this season by about seven or eight points!"

I can honestly say it was one of the most enjoyable interviews I've ever conducted. That's not a disrespect to the players I've spoken to, who have all been lovely and a pleasure to talk to. But Danny and Elsie are both eloquent, enthusiastic and engaged speakers, and it seems strange that they both claim to hate the limelight. Indeed, that's one of the reasons they haven't given interviews before - they'd rather keep their love for Luton quiet, rather than bragging about their commitment. I'm not sure who's more surprised, me or them, when their names appear in the pages of The Sun the following week, with a little article which appears to have been based directly on mine. Imitation is the sincerest form of flattery, and all that, I suppose...

Hartlepool home - Marvin for England!

I feel dreadful. I had to interview Steve Howard last week (who laughed a lot when I asked him if he did indeed commit a handball against Hartlepool away - when he recovered himself, he said, "I was going to! I definitely went to do something with it! Then I thought, 'Oh my God, I canna do that!'" He denied fouling the keeper for the first goal that day as well, and having watched the replay on TV I have to agree with him when he said, "No, I went for the ball, and the keeper was watching me instead of watching the ball, and just took his eye off it"). When I arrived at the club he had a streaming cold and did not seem very well at all (and yet he still manages to play every game. Some other squad members would do well to learn from him). Now I appear to have caught a sniffle, which I am now going to suffer all over Christmas, and it's horrible.

Clearly though I can't miss a game. And I am glad that I don't.

Marvin Johnson has sometimes taken stick from fans, but he's certainly a cult figure now. He's our longest serving player, and certainly has his footballing shortcomings. He has been with us over our years of decline, and been a major part in the headless chicken defences during our relegation seasons. However, it has to be borne in mind that the teams he was playing in were very poor, and no one could possibly have shone in those line ups. Maybe this season, with two of the fantastic Perrett, Bayliss (who we've just signed on a short term contract) or Coyne (who suffered a knee injury last week, the day after he became a father for the first time) in the middle, it was thought that perhaps Marv could finally prove his ability at left back. Not only that, maybe he might also get a chance to go on some of those weaving, mazy runs into the opposition's half for which he is renowned.

It would be nice, but sadly Marv is now too old and too injury prone to be a regular member of the team. At the moment, he's match fit, so he's a constant presence on the bench. We can be forgiven, then, for not expecting him to change the game when he comes on towards the end of the second half.

But he does. A wonderful shot from the edge of the box means that Marv salvages us a point. Thanks, Marv, and Merry Christmas to you too.

Oxford away

A reasonably close away fixture for Boxing Day, so my dad, my sister, Graham and I pile in the car and nip down the road to the shiny new Kassam Stadium.

Ah, the Kassam Stadium, named after Oxford's chairman. Joe, as Oxford's former Director of Football, gave his verdict on it a while back, when he declared that anybody naming a stadium after themselves would have to be a complete prat. He also pronounced all the Oxford fans "muppets", and said that he would bare his backside in Harrods' window should Oxford finish above us this season. So this is another fixture we have to win to protect Joe's pride.

We do, easy peasy, 2-1. Two and a half thousand Luton fans pack into the side stand (for some reason they haven't built a stand behind one of the goals yet) and see an excellent all round team performance. Throughout the game, we look dangerous going forward, Matty Taylor having an exceptional game, and Valois threatening to live up to expectation. Our central defence pairing of Perrett and Bayliss is impressive - level headed, sensible and with a fair amount of skill each, they give me some sort of confidence in our back four. Despite this, Oxford take the lead (undeservedly, in my opinion) when a poor square ball from Nicholls fails to reach the falling Boyce, and then Ovendale comes off his line when really he has no need to do so. We have the better of the first half, I think, and this is emphasised just a few minutes after Oxford's goal, when their keeper has to make two very good point blank saves from headers from first Howard then Bayliss. We get back on terms just before half time, when what looks a rather soft shot from Crowie goes past the keeper's reach. Our second comes just after half time, with Spring finishing off a beautifully worked move, worthy of winning any game.

We're second in the table, and only three points behind Plymouth. All is well.

Southend away

A modicum of revenge for our Cup exit at their hands, and we complete our first "double" of the season. Our first team are back. We go in 0-0 at the break; although we're looking good going forward down the left, the final ball just isn't there. After half time, we switch to a more defensive formation - Forbes and Valois are replaced with Hillier and Brkovic. Yet we manage to concede a goal shortly after the restart, after Hills is roasted down the left hand side. The inevitable equaliser comes from Crowe after good work from Howard, and we snatch the win with a close range side foot by Taylor. Not a pretty display, but an effective one, and another valuable win.

Villa 2 Man Utd 3

It's the Christmas holidays, and so I'm temping again. This time, I'm working as a data entry clerk in a Central London accountants'. It's straightforward stuff, if a little boring, and the only real drawback with the job (and temping in general) is that I don't know anyone in the office. So at lunchtime I sit at my desk, eat my sandwich and check my email.

On Friday, I have an email from Mark, who tells me that Ladbrokes' online betting have given him a free £20 bet on the result of the weekend's FA Cup Third Round game between Manchester United and Aston Villa, and asks me for my prediction. Bearing in mind the dodgy defences of both sides, I plump for 3-2 to Man United, and mail him back immediately. He replies saying that 3-2 is at odds of 25/1, so he'll go for it, and if it comes in then we'll split it half and half. Sounds a good deal to me.

The game is televised on the Sunday evening, and after a goalless first half the bet is beginning to look unlikely. Mark texts me to say: "DON'T WORRY. 5 GLS IN 2ND HALF." And within the first fifteen minutes of the second half, we're halfway there, as Villa go two up, with a goal from Ian Taylor and an own goal from Phil Neville. Then United get one back. Then they equalise. Then in the 82nd minute, they go ahead. As soon as the net bulges with van Nistlerooy's strike, my phone rings, and Mark is shouting, "I can't watch, I can't watch, I'm going down the pub!" I decide to switch over to the Pete Waterman documentary on Channel 5, but can't resist flicking over to check that the score is still the same. I wander round my room, rearranging my CDs, and am surprised to hear myself muttering, "Please let it stay at 3-2. Please let it stay at 3-2." I channel-hop again, back to the game, and it's in injury time...and then it's all over! My phone rings again, and Mark and I are both screaming, "We won five hundred quid!"

We meet up the next day, big grins on our faces, conversation consisting primarily of us going, "We won five hundred quid!" Mark says that he couldn't sleep because he was worried he hadn't put the bet on correctly, and if he hadn't he would have given me £250 anyway as he wouldn't have been able to confess that he'd messed it up.

I do feel a bit guilty from profiting from a Manchester United victory, as obviously I hate them as does any other self respecting lower league fan, but in the end, who really cares?

Kidderminster away

This is the game that was postponed at the start of December. We owe this lot a thrashing. That will teach them to doubt the might and the honesty of Super Luton Town.

We cruise it, 4-1. After Kiddy take the lead, we are undoubtedly assisted by Kidderminster's dodgy keeper, one Stuart Brock, who helps us by missing crosses, failing to hold onto balls, throwing himself over the top of shots. If my sister was here, she'd be crying at the abuse that is being hurled his way and his total inadequacy to deal with shots, crosses or kicking.

Villain of the piece, apart from whinging Jan Molby (who is serenaded by the song, "Molby, what's your weight, Molby, Molby, what's your weight?"), is Drewe Broughton, Kiddy's striker. Ironically he is a Luton fan - in fact, his brother Gregg is on my mailing list. Broughton is a big, bustling centre forward, all arms and legs, and commits the sin of whacking Nico in the face. Perhaps Nico is finally growing up, because he manages to contain his temper and not punch the fella back, as he so richly deserves. When Broughton also hits Perrett, though, Nico does use some choice phrases, directed at the ref, along the lines of, "Mr Referee, sir, how many more times are you going to let him get away with that?" On the whole, though, he and the team let their football do the talking. Brilliant stuff on a cold Tuesday night.

Cheltenham away; Steve Howard.

To say that Luton fans have not adjusted well to being in Division Three would be an understatement. We believe that we are intrinsically superior to everyone else in the lower echelons of the League. With our vocal certainty that our residence in Division Three is only temporary, we have managed to annoy the fans of pretty much every other club, inevitably resulting in arguments and threats of handbags (just ask Plymouth and Oxford).

The bitching directed at our own players has been more depressing. This has occurred because something else to which we haven't adjusted is watching players who aren't as talented as the members of our Eighties' glory teams. Joe Kinnear's first signing is the finest example of this - striker Steve Howard, formerly of Hartlepool and Tow Law Town, signed from Northampton for £50,000 in the midst of last season's relegation battle.

For most of the dismal 2000-2001 season, every fan at Kenilworth Road was bemoaning the lack of physical presence up front. We have a grand tradition of the target man/goal poacher combination; every English fan over a certain age will, I'm sure, remember Mick Harford and Brian Stein's partnership throughout the Eighties. So when the 6'3", 13 stone Howard was signed last March, it was assumed that he was the man who would make the difference to our team and score the goals to keep us in Division Two.

It was not to be. Despite Howard's penalty at Colchester and his spectacular lob from the halfway line at Brentford, the damage had already been done. Besides which, we couldn't defend to save our lives; no matter how many goals we scored there was no way we'd ever stop the opposition from scoring more. Howard's incredible work rate had been noted but a certain section of fans took against him, resenting him for not keeping us up single-handedly and disregarding his off the ball work as irrelevant. At the start of this season, his prolific new strike partner, Carl Griffiths, was quick to pay tribute to the contribution of Howie. Yet those fans who were against Howard dismissed Griff's comments as "dressing room spin" (clearly the PR at Kenilworth Road is a strong rival to Millbank), and Howard's lack of goals did nothing to convince them that he was a useful member of the side.

The crunch came with that York away game. After that, you were either for Howie or against him, and I'm sad to say most people were against. As I've said, I was not one of this majority. When we first signed Howie, I took a liking to his no-nonsense, uncompromising style of play. The events of September and the subsequent onslaught of abuse meant that he's gone from being my nominal favourite player to "my" player (an honour accorded to only one other player in recent years, that being Tony Thorpe). After nagging Geoff, as I've mentioned I was allowed to interview Steve Howard just before Christmas, and asked him if he felt that any of the criticism he'd received had been justified. He answered that he didn't mind getting criticism about his goal-scoring record, because he knew he ought to get more, but as long as he worked hard, and as long as his dad and the Gaffer were pleased with him, then he thought he was doing OK. Quite shocked at his pragmatic attitude (especially bearing in mind how irate I was getting with some of the people on the terraces), I asked him if criticism really didn't bother him. He replied that it didn't, he could cope with it, and that I shouldn't worry about it either. In return, I told that there were a lot of us who watched the game properly and appreciated his contribution, and I knew he'd come good and get more goals.

I wish to take partial credit, then, for Howard's fantastic form since Christmas. He's got loads more goals (and he's now well on his way to surpassing his previous goalscoring record, which was ten in Northampton's Division Three promotion season), and was unanimously voted Man of the Match today against Cheltenham. Even the most vocal and vitriolic Howard-bashers have been forced to eat their words (or rather Howie has rammed them down their throats). The more reasonable ones, who objected to his poor goal-scoring record while recognising his value to the team, have gone so far as to issue an apology to him. It was lovely at Kidderminster three days ago, when the entire away terrace sang his name at the end of the game, to his obvious pleasure.

At the end of the season, no doubt Luton fans will be speculating on who has been Joe Kinnear's best signing. And I expect the names that will be mentioned most often will be Taylor for his fine attacking play, Valois for his Gallic flair, and Nico for his bone crunching tackles that make me wince every time he gets near a player. But even now, I know I would nominate Howie, no matter what happens for the rest of the season. He stayed here at Luton and proved his critics wrong when it would have been so easy to walk away. His shooting may still occasionally leave a little bit to be desired, but his enthusiasm, commitment, work rate and will to win are second to none. Steve Howard - I salute you.

Carlisle home

A disappointing draw against a Carlisle team in good form. We just don't have our shooting boots on - if we'd gone in at half time three goals ahead, it would have been a fair reflection of the play. As it is, we have to equalise through a Russ Perrett header after sixty-seven minutes. This point, though, could prove invaluable: Plymouth lose to Shrewsbury, and now we are just one point behind them. On the other hand, these two dropped points could prove decisive in what looks like will be an extremely close race to the title. It's more than a little irritating to think that if we had won today, as we probably deserved, we'd be top.

The League Cup

Tonight is the second leg of the Worthington Cup semi-finals. With so many fixtures, the top clubs (who make the ridiculously fixed and protracted European competitions their priority now) usually put out a second string team in the League Cup, leading to much debate over whether it should continue in its current form. Tottenham thrash Chelsea, coming back from a first leg deficit to win 6-3 on aggregate. I am surprised to hear an Arsenal-supporting friend of mine declare that if Spurs win the Worthington Cup, he will laugh because it will just emphasise the gap between the two North London clubs - Arsenal can get a place in Europe because they finish high enough in the league, and Tottenham have to rely on a rubbish cup competition for a UEFA Cup spot. I disagree totally, but then I would, wouldn't I? I'm a Luton fan, and the League Cup holds very special memories for us. We were banned from competing in the competition in 1986-87 because our chairman at the time, David Evans MP, refused to lift our away fans ban (instituted after the infamous Millwall riot of 1985). We were reinstated in 1987-88, and were determined to prove a point. As always on these occasions, my mind drifts back to a sunny Saturday afternoon in April, nearly fourteen years ago now.

I was eight at the time, and mad keen to go to football. After Luton had beaten Oxford in the two-legged semi-final of what was then the Littlewoods Cup, my dad bought two tickets for Wembley, and I was convinced that one of them was for me. Even when he told me that it wasn't, I thought he was just joking - after all, surely he'd let me go to a Cup Final?

No, he wouldn't. The day of April 24th dawned, and I realised that my dad wasn't teasing me. The second ticket was not for me at all, but for my dad's mate, Anthony. (Ant is a purely nominal Luton fan, by his own admission, and I have never forgiven him for taking that ticket. I still mention it occasionally - something along the lines of, "You know when you took that ticket for the Cup Final and left me psychologically scarred?" - and he feels suitably guilty.) They set off for Wembley, and I stayed at home to watch the game live on television.

We were playing the mighty Arsenal, and of course we were underdogs. Arsenal were the defending Cup-holders, with a team full of Englishmen (quite commonplace at the time, unheard of now), most of whom were or would one day be internationals. We, on the other hand, were without our first choice goalkeeper, Les Sealey, who had concussion from the previous League match. He was replaced by his deputy, Andy Dibble. Our manager, Ray Harford, had some trickier selections to make in midfield. Should he pick Ricky Hill, just recovered from a broken leg? What about teenager Kingsley Black, just nineteen? The answer, he decided, was "yes" to both questions, and the team lined up as follows:

Andy Dibble; Tim Breacker, Rob Johnson, Mal Donaghy, Steve Foster; Danny Wilson, David Preece, Ricky Hill, Kingsley Black; Brian Stein, Mick Harford.

Subs: Mark Stein, Ashley Grimes. (Those were the days...only two subs!)

What followed had to be one of the most exciting games seen at Wembley in recent years, if not ever. Stein senior scored on 13 minutes, taking us in at half time one-nil up. Arsenal began to assert themselves at the beginning of the second half, scoring twice in the space of five minutes, and when they were awarded a penalty (totally unjustly) it looked like our Wembley dream was about to be dashed.

So Nigel Winterburn stepped up, with the chance to make it 3-1 to Arsenal and put the game beyond our reach...and Dibble, at full stretch, tipped his shot round the post. If you've got the video recorded straight from the TV at the time, you can actually hear Dibble go, "Oof!" as he gets his hand to it. The corner is cleared, and Luton are revived. Danny Wilson's stooping header on 82 minutes brings us level, and as the ninety-minute mark grows ever nearer, Stein bags his second of the game, our third, and the Cup.

We didn't get a place in Europe. English clubs were banned from participating in European club competitions after the Heysel disaster, and so we were robbed of our chance to grace the European stage. You can't help but feel sorry for class players, international players, like Harford, Stein and Foster, who at that time would have been a match for anyone, but never got a chance to prove themselves against the very best. It really touched me when I read an interview with our tiny midfielder, David Preece, in a magazine about ten years ago, and he said that he was very sad that Mick Harford and Brian Stein didn't get more England caps as they were a lethal partnership. "I don't care what anyone says, those two were running at defences and tearing them apart," were his exact words. Still, they got to climb the steps at Wembley and receive a winner's medal, which doesn't happen to many people.

So I disagree with the tabloid hacks that have dubbed the Worthington Cup "the Worthless Cup". I think the big clubs should be made to take it seriously and to treat such a grand old competition with respect. I appreciate that now they also have to compete in Europe, but they get more than adequate financial reward for that - if they whine about fixture congestion affecting their players, they can damn well go out and buy more players and start a squad rotation system. Why should the rest of us suffer a second-rate competition because of a bunch of overpaid prima donnas?

Darlington away

Another 500 mile round trip, another early start. The London Transport system today manages to be vaguely efficient, unlike the Hartlepool debacle, but then I do set out on my journey nearly three hours later. Geoff offered me a lift again, planning to leave South Woodford around 9. I caught an 8am bus from Camberwell Green, got to Liverpool Street for 8.30am, straight on to the tube, and in the car at 9am. Fantastic. Thank you, London Transport.

One advantage of not driving is that I can go to sleep during long journeys. This is particularly good today. It was my friend Susan's birthday celebration last night, which involved various pubs and then a club on Shaftesbury Avenue. Coming from Luton, where the pubs kick you out at 11.30 on the dot, and the clubs close at 2, I forget that clubs in London basically never close. At 3am I realised what the time was and that I had to be up in four hours, and legged it out to the bus stop, where a night bus was waiting for me. (That's a good thing about London Transport - buses. They run fairly regularly over twenty four hours - how cool is that?)

So I manage three hours' sleep. And then, inevitably and rather embarrassingly, I fall asleep in the passenger seat halfway up the M1, until I am woken up by Geoff laughing at me because my phone's ringing. Oh well. At least I didn't fall asleep during the match. Although perhaps it might have been better if I had done so.

Feethams, Darlington's ground, is a funny little place, with a 'paddock' standing area which is just in front of the wooden side stand where the away fans are seated. Because I'm so early, and get into the ground at quarter to two, I manage to get a spot on the terrace dead on the halfway line, right at the front. Although there's posts obscuring my view of two corners, I have a great view of our first goal, a brilliantly taken Howie header from a beautiful Valois corner, and then our second, a magnificent Valois strike from a great pass by Brkovic (who, incidentally, is the latest victim of the boo-boys. Why - I don't know. Certainly Berky is not the most spectacular of players, but then you don't always need spectacular. With the mercurial Valois on one side of the midfield, Berky is a steadying influence on the other. I'm not quite sure why certain fans believe their knowledge of the game is superior to Joe's.) 1-0 up, then 2-1 up, and we manage to throw it away in the last ten minutes, primarily due to panicking amongst our makeshift defence. We lose 3-2, I am exhausted, and my sore throat is beginning to develop into yet another cold.

As the terraces empty at the end of the game, I notice the dozens of posters along the walls - "Vote for Zoe!" Of course, it's the latest reality TV phenomenon, Pop Idol, and Darlington girl Zoe Birkett is one of the four contenders left in the competition. How I love that show. I never really got into Popstars (the show which spawned the evil that is Hear'Say), but I absolutely adore Pop Idol. Partly of course this is due to the brilliant Ant and Dec, and partly because of the bitching between the judges (particularly Simon Cowell and Pete Waterman), but also because I love to listen to people perform all kinds of music. This programme has come in for a bit of stick for making the contestants sing different styles of songs (recent themes have been big band music and Abba), but I think versatility is so important in understanding the developments which have led to pop music today. Also singing different types of song has a positive influence in increasing a performer's musicality.

I've been thinking about this a lot recently, and I do think that history is important whatever line of work you're in. And (didn't you just know it) I think it's a relevant point to apply to football. When Joe Kinnear first took over at Luton, there were fears that he would make us play the long-ball game, which is popularly associated with Wimbledon, the club at which he made his managerial name. Luton's tradition is that of the pretty passing game, ball to feet, usually with two wingers flying down the flanks knocking in inch-perfect crosses. And to our delight (and perhaps surprise) Joe has continued playing this type of game. But maybe it helps that Luton is a club that also has a tradition of keeping ex-players on as coaches. Mick Harford is the first team coach, Brian Stein is in charge of the reserves, and John Moore runs the youth team. Players know that their coaches have set the fans' standards and expectations that they must now live up to. Yet Joe brings with him a reputation for ruthlessness and directness - pretty football is no good without an end result. Division Three isn't the place for Total Football, it's full of cloggers, kids on their way up, veterans at the end of their career. It's a contact sport, and for all our desire to play the passing game, we have to make certain concessions towards physicality. So there's the other parallel - you have to learn from different methods of performing in order to be truly successful.

So much for my theory. What went wrong today? Maybe we need just a bit more rehearsal.

Andrew Fotiadis

The first official London crew outing of the New Year. This time we're going to watch the reserves play at Brentford's Griffin Park. I meet Kev at Waterloo Platform 15 at quarter past five, and we take the train to Brentford.

Griffin Park is probably most famous for having a pub on each of the four corners of the ground. We have about an hour to kill before kick off at 7, so we have a few drinks in The Griffin, which is a nice little place. Mark and his Brentford-supporting mate Tony arrive at about twenty to seven, in time to get a round in, then we cross the road in the pouring rain to take our places in the front row of the main stand.

Our reserves aren't very good. It's a similar line-up to the one that faced Dagenham in the LDV Trophy. About half of them are under 21, and about half are remnants of last year's squad that got us relegated. We've also got three triallists playing. Surprisingly though we manage to make a lot of chances, but our spectacularly inept strike force does not convert any of them.

This is because one half of tonight's strike pairing is Andrew Fotiadis. Now, I am not saying that Foti is a bad player, because he isn't. He's a local lad (born and bred in Hitchin), and came through the ranks, having a startling first few games in which he scored some great goals - one in particular sticks in my mind, a sensational volley from the edge of the box against Walsall, in 1996.

Foti was 18 then. He's 24 now. He's scored 14 goals in 123

first team appearances (although a good proportion of those were as sub). Bearing in mind his undoubted talent and his prodigious goalscoring ability demonstrated in those first few games, you would have thought that he would have established himself as a first team regular and probably later secured himself a big money move to a higher division team - as his almost-contemporaries Gary Doherty, Paul McLaren and John Hartson did.

However, his career has been blighted with injuries. That's injuries, plural. Of course I sympathise with any player who suffers with a series of long-term injuries, but that's never been the case with Foti. His ailments are usually of an inane kind - a hamstring tweak, a broken finger, a fractured eyelash. OK, the last was a joke, but you get the picture. Perhaps I'm being harsh on him, but I don't think so. The broken finger particularly annoyed me because people kept stressing that it was a really bad break. Well, dear me. Brian Stein scored two goals in the League Cup Final with a bloody plaster cast on his arm, so forgive me if I think it's reasonable to expect someone to play with a broken finger. Some players pull a muscle and play on through their injury because they're so desperate to be a successful professional footballer and won't let a minor pain distract them. Others get more serious injuries, say a torn ligament, and they will work their backsides off in order to get back to match fitness. But Foti fits into neither of these categories. His injuries are consecutive and seemingly interminable. Joe Kinnear was impressed with Foti when he first arrived at the club (despite having problems pronouncing his name, so much so that he resorted to calling Foti "the other lad", as in "Liam George, Stuart Douglas and the other lad") and gave him a new contract. He now seems to be running out of patience with him, making cutting comments like, "He made it through the reserve game so he might be in contention for a squad place, but we'll have to wait and see with him because he could wake up injured." The Dagenham game in the LDV Trophy must have done nothing to improve Joe's opinion of his misfit striker.

Tonight would have been no different. Brian Stein gave Foti and Peter Thomson both a rollicking after the reserves lost to amateur team Wootton Blue Cross in the Bedfordshire Senior Cup last week, saying that professionals who performed so badly against enthusiastic amateurs really should be shot. Steiny also commented on Foti's red card in the same game, which he pronounced "the best thing he did all evening". You would think that any professional with a modicum of pride and belief in his own abilities would go out and give 100% in order to prove his manager wrong.

Foti's not like that. He seems to think he has nothing to prove, and plays like reserve football is beneath him. It's common knowledge that he finished school with a few A-levels and was considering going to university, but decided to embark on his football career - a decision, by all accounts, he apparently regrets. It's a scary thought that some (clearly insane and/or stupid) Luton fans think he ought to be in the first team. What has he done to prove his worth for selection? His goalscoring form isn't prolific, even at reserve level, he doesn't appear to care enough about whatever game he's playing in, he clearly can't train impressively hard, and he's never fully fit. I agree that he is a very talented player, but what's the use if he can't, or even sadder doesn't want to, apply his talent? I'm afraid that tonight is the final straw for me with Foti. At the age of 24, he ought to have at least learnt a professional attitude by now, and that doesn't seem to be the case. Players who don't pull their weight and pick up pay cheques each week while doing nothing in return are part of the reason that Luton Town are now in Division Three, and I will shed no tears if his contract is terminated in the summer.

On the plus side, we retire first to the supporters' bar underneath the main stand, where Geoff joins us, and stay there till we get kicked out. We then wander round to the next pub which is blessed with a juke box full of fabulous 80s songs, so we are forced to feed it pound coins and establish the play list for the rest of the evening. The delicious pints of Grolsch served in Middlesex inspire Kev to write the following ditty in honour of our very own Sicknote, to be sung to the tune of "That's Amore":

He couldn't score in a Tardis,
He don't know what a yard is,
Fot-i-a-dis!

His ancestors are Greek,
His career's up shit creek,
Fot-i-a-dis!

The fact that Foti is actually of Cypriot descent does not in my view detract from the genius of this work. Neither does the fact that, when he wakes up the next morning, Kev cannot remember writing these lyrics at all.

Plymouth home

The biggest game of the season so far. First against second. The best attack against the best defence. The three points on offer today could eventually prove the difference between an automatic promotion spot and the Championship.

A rather distressing characteristic of mine is that I get extremely nervous before big games, so much so that my sub-conscious is subsumed by my waking football preoccupation and I end up dreaming entire games. On Friday night I dream that we lose 3-1 to Plymouth, and Ian Hillier is sent off. When I wake up on Saturday morning I am even more worried about the ninety minutes to come.

I log on to the message board and read some posts claiming that the main stand roof has taken the brunt of some strong winds over the past 48 hours, and the fire brigade has been inspecting the stadium for health and safety hazards. I actually believe this in hindsight totally obvious wind-up, because I am incredibly gullible, so I text Kev and Mark, both travelling in from London. (I'm at my parents' as I went clubbing with my little sister on Thursday night - Chesney Hawkes, he of "The One and Only" fame, was playing in Dunstable!) Three minutes later I text them both back apologising for my idiotically credulous nature. Not a good start.

We arrive at Kenilworth Road, and there are three team changes from last week. Embo replaces Ovengloves in goal,

Bayliss is back from his suspension, and Forbesy starts instead of Berky. We're obviously going for it - start with all-out attack, running at the notoriously competent Pilgrims' defence. It's shaping up to be a great afternoon - Plymouth are one of the very few clubs to have sold out the Oak Road End, and the 2,000 travelling fans are making lots of noise.

The first half is so incredibly one-sided even I can't believe it. We create dozens of chances, but miss each and every one. Valois gets the ball in the net at one point, but it's disallowed for a foul on the keeper, prompting my dad's traditional reminiscence about the good old days when you were allowed to push the keeper in the back of the net along with the ball. Plymouth are obviously excellent defensively, but they are very negative and have clearly come here with the plan of not losing.

The trouble with being a Luton fan is that you're used to disappointment. There have been literally hundreds of games where we are all over the opposition, doing everything but score, and then the other team attack us on the break and nick a goal, from which we can't come back. I say to my sister at half time that if we don't score in the first fifteen minutes of the second half, then Plymouth would grab a half chance and proceed to shut up shop on us. She tells me to be quiet.

Sixty minutes on the clock, and it's still nil-nil. My hopes of a famous victory begin to fade. Forbesy has a shot that may have crossed the line, but it isn't given. I begin to think that eventually we may rue all our missed chances. And then Taylor runs into the box, is hacked down, and the penalty is given, right in front of the Luton fans.

The Kenny End goes mad - shouting and screaming and swearing. I can't think of a more tense moment in recent Lutonian history. Nil nil, and we have a penalty with just fifteen minutes left. Brave Kevin Nicholls steps up. I can't watch - I turn away from the pitch and cover my face with my hands. It's almost as nerve wracking not watching such a crucial penalty; it's definitely worse seeing what happens, but listening to it is dreadful. It's always the same successions of sounds. The whistle blows and a silence descends. The whack of the boot on the ball. Silence again - and the anticipation of a huge cheer from one end or the other, depending on the success of the kick. And the Luton fans erupt! Hugging and cheering, and the players are ecstatic.

A slender lead, but I'm now sure we'll hang on. The win is assured by my Howie, who powers home a close range header on 86 minutes to put us two-nil up. The "all action hit man" (description courtesy of the News of the World) runs to salute the delirious Kenny End, kisses his shirt and blows us a kiss (although I'm sure it's really directed at me, being his number one fan and all). Mark's chant at Darlington of "Feed the Howie and he will score" now seems very apposite - four goals in five for him now, and twelve in forty one Luton appearances. That's not bad going, especially bearing in mind that he's never played as a primary goalscorer before and went through a two month dry spell at the start of the season.

After the final whistle, the players applaud the fans, and we reciprocate. A fantastic footballing performance, such a difference from last week's debacle. I'm so proud of the boys. Mark and I decide to celebrate with a few drinks in a local pub (Kev declines to join us as he has a prior engagement) and we get chatting to some Plymouth fans. They're really nice, very reasonable and they have decent opinions on the game. Surely this is what football should all be about - travelling round the country following your team, watching an excellent game, then an evening of discussing the game (and the state of the railways, and Pop Idol) with the opposition fans.

Rochdale away

Talking of railways, Mark and I have a new game, developed after the "few drinks" post-Plymouth game. We adopted a phrase from someone's message board posting, "Super Speedo Stevo Howard" and for some reason which now eludes me decided to adapt it into a nickname for the Thameslink train service us London dwellers use to get to home games - "Superhowie Express". The new game is then to change the names of stations into ones of Luton players past and present - for example Leagrave becomes Lee-Mansell-grave, and West Hampstead Thameslink becomes Alan West Hampstead Thameslink. We find it endlessly entertaining and the source of great amusement. (I think of the best one, however, when we extend the game to include tube stations - Highbury & Islington becomes Highbury & Des Linton. Do you get it?)

As we make the trip to Rochdale, we change the game again - any roadsign or advert or logo on a lorry can now be converted into names of people with Luton connections. It passes the time, anyway, as we make the three-hour trek up the motorway, although I'm not quite sure my sister understands how inherently funny the game is.

The football game, though, is not funny at all. Another awful referee (yes, I mean you, Mr Matthew Messias) ruins the game by booking everyone in sight and blowing his whistle every thirty seconds. Nico is booked in the first five minutes so can't put a tackle in for the rest of the game, leaving his man to waltz clear of all our players and score a flukey deflected goal in the twelfth minute. Despite us having the majority of the possession for the rest of the game, we don't get a goal. The icing of the cake is the sending off of David Bayliss, making a return to the club he left on less-than-amiable terms just before Christmas. It's so frustrating. How can a team that tore apart the league leaders one week look like they could play till next week and not score today?

So we sulk all the way home. Pip's brought her battery powered TV with her (a free gift from one of the banks that bribe students to open accounts with them) but we can't get a signal to watch the Pop Idol final. Luckily I get home in time to watch the results at quarter past ten - and the underdog Will is triumphant. Another shock. Maybe there's another music and football analogy to be drawn here, about the dangers of complacency and people making assumptions and the underdog's determination...but I'm too angry to bother.

Scunthorpe home, my birthday party.

I was born on the 15th February, 1980, in Luton (obviously). Today is the day after my 22nd birthday, and my friends and I have got tickets for the Century Club, the exclusive fans' club for supporters who stump up huge amounts of cash year in year out. Of course, Danny sorted us out these tickets, and there's seven of us entering the world of match day hospitality today - me, my sister, Mark, Kev and Scotty (from my mailing list), and Claire and Caren, my best friends from university. Whilst the first five of us are committed and dedicated Luton fans and followers of football (well, Scotty's a referee who trains the Premier League refs, which is almost the same), the latter two are not. Caren has been to a few games before, but this is all entirely new to Claire, whose boyfriend plays rugby in front of relatively small crowds, so she's looking forward to seeing around 6,000 people in Kenilworth Road.

We get to the ground just before one, which is when the players turn up. Nico is one of the first there, and he says hello to me - everyone else is suitably impressed. Marvin Johnson, our esteemed but terminally injured club captain (he's 33 now), is stopped at the door and asked for his pass to get into the ground; as he's not playing and not part of the matchday squad he needs a ticket to get in. He doesn't look very happy.

Our performance today is pretty dreadful. We lose 3-2 in the last minute, after twice equalising. We have Chris Coyne, a centre half, playing at full back, and Gary McSwegan, a Scot who has played in the Champions' League with Rangers, making his debut for us whilst clearly not match fit. The day would have been a total let down had it not been for:

a) the fantastic Century Club hospitality. Free food, tea, coffee, and a lovely bar, complete with birthday champagne for me.
b) the fine company. Thanks, boys and girls.
c) Caren and Claire's honest enjoyment of what I suppose was a fairly exciting game for the neutral.

In The Century Club
L-R Kev, Caren, Claire, your Author

Both of them quickly pick up on nicknames and are conversing about "Howie, Nico and Forbesy" with the rest of us. And both of them establish their favourite players - Caren takes a liking to Jean Louis Valois, and Claire to Adrian Forbes. In fact, Claire provides what is probably the highlight of the whole day. When some bloke behind us starts moaning at Forbesy, she turns round and says, "Do you mind? He's having a great game. And by the way, he's my husband." Of course, there's no way you can respond to that, and while we are all in hysterics, the bloke is suitably humbled. Talking about this comment later, Claire enquires of us, "But that was a good thing to say, wasn't it?" When we assure her that it was fantastic, she is pleased, and pronounces it "the funniest thing I've ever said".

Scotty, Caren and Claire leave straight after the game due to prior engagements, leaving Mark, Kev, Pip and me in the bar, musing over ways to exact our revenge on the players. As more alcohol is consumed, the more outlandish the plots become. For example, Mark asks Kev if he has his lighter with him. When Kev replies in the negative and that he's given up smoking today, Mark is disappointed, and says, "Well, have you got any form of inflammable material? We need to set fire to Matthew Spring." Harsh but fair.

We go on to one of Luton's finest curry houses, Balti Nights, and eat and drink lots. Mark tries to pick a fight with a waiter who has proclaimed himself a Liverpool fan. We also write another verse of our Foti song:

> *His efforts are puny,*
> *He'd rather go to uni,*
> *Fot-i-a-dis!*

Then on to Jumpin' Jaks, the finest nightclub in Dunstable, where we meet up with some old friends of mine - Katy, Mike, Duncan (all from school) and Rob. Pip, Mark and I keep screeching, "He's my HUSBAND!" and reducing ourselves to helpless giggles, then our mood swings and we sit there and spit out, "Matthew Spring," in vitriolic tones.

Despite the players' best efforts to ruin it, then, I have a really good day. It would be nice if, just for once, Luton could manage to win the game nearest to my birthday. It's getting ridiculous now.

February 19th, 2002

Bristol Rovers home

The problem with British winters is that we always get games postponed over Christmas. This one is a rearrangement due to Rovers' Cup commitments at the beginning of January (and luckily the postponement meant that I could go to Gary's birthday party on time after all). I like midweek games as a rule, but when it's cold, dark, and I have to get back to Denmark Hill afterwards, it's a bit of a chore.

The trials of being an impoverished Luton fan are always made much easier to bear when we turn out accomplished performances resulting in comprehensive victories. The players have obviously taken long hard looks at themselves after Saturday's debacle, and the team, despite consisting of fundamentally the same players, is unrecognisable. A solid display, an easy 3-0 win, with goals from Howard, Coyne and Nicholls, who scores from a penalty after Howard is chopped down and Rovers are reduced to 10 men. The three-goal margin of victory means that due to our superior goal difference we're back in second place. The promotion train is back on track.

February 23rd, 2002

York home

We've been a bit unlucky with injuries so far this season. As soon as Chris Coyne returns to form after his knee ligament injury, we lose Russ Perrett, and then David Bayliss, meaning that our defence has a makeshift look about it. Joe has brought in loan signing Alan Neilson to partner Coyne in the middle, and he makes his debut today.

If there was any justice in the world, we'd win 2-0, with a brace of penalties both scored by Howie. As it is, we win 2-1, with a brace from open play both scored by Howie, one in each half. The first is a majestic header, the second a little fortunate as his downward header bounces back onto his knee and from there into the net. At last, the ghost of York is exorcised for him, as he extends his lead in the club's top scorers chart, with 13 overall.

Lincoln away

After beating Bristol Rovers and York at home, we now have our first away game since the debacle at Rochdale. The problem is, it's another silly Tuesday night game. Not because Lincoln is a long way away, because it's not, but because I've got a seminar at university that doesn't finish until three, and my dad's planning to set out from Dunstable at half past two.

I call upon the chauffeur service of Geoff again, who picks me up at four. We navigate our way through the diversions on the A505 and make it to Lincoln with an hour and a half to spare, in spite of Geoff's ridiculously pessimistic proclamations that "we might be cutting it a bit fine". My dad and sister are already settled in the supporters' clubhouse, where I join them in chatting to some friendly Imps. I do like games where there's no atmosphere of menace, where you can sit down and have a drink with the opposition fans.

Anyway, the game is nothing to get excited about (we win 1-0, with a goal from Taylor right on the stroke of half time), and it's freezing cold. Some stupid men behind me have decided to sit outside on a February evening in shirtsleeves, and they wonder why they're feeling the chill. They whinge all the way through the second half and start calling for the ref to blow his whistle with twenty minutes still to play. Idiots.

Torquay away

But Torquay, on the other hand, is a beautiful, golden place, with the sun shining down on us. Although I am always prepared for inclement weather (and as such am clutching my woolly hat, suede gloves, fleece and jacket) it is so warm that I have no need to put on any extra layers. I bask in the sunshine on the terrace directly behind the goal, and am in the perfect spot to see Ahmet Brkovic score his first league goal for us, which turns out to be the winner.

My dad is driving a hire car today, with me, Graham and Mark as his passengers. After the game, we drive down to the seafront, and descend on a dinky little beach shop. I buy boxes of Devon Cream Fudge (which I am ashamed to say I eat before I get back to London), Mark buys a postcard of local landmark Thatcher's Rock as a gift for his determinedly socialist flatmate, and my dad very kindly buys me an ice cream, fighting off offers from Graham and Mark to pay for it. Bless.

It's just a shame we won't be coming here next season.

Leyton Orient home

These three-nil midweek home wins are getting to be a very nice habit now. Dean Crowe breaks his duck this year by notching one in the second half, after Chris Coyne opens the scoring. Forbesy wraps it up just after the hour. The downside is the injury to a marvellously in-form Kevin Nicholls, who tries to play on with a heavily strapped ankle but has to be substituted. Unfortunately he has to walk the perimeter of the pitch to reach the tunnel, and goes past the Orient fans. They hurl abuse, and Nico is not known for his placid temperament. According to Orient supporters, he makes a gesture at them and they are all going to complain to the FA, because it's just **NOT FAIR.**

Supporters are a funny bunch. They see it as quite normal to shout offensive comments to players, and then they're outraged when players respond in kind. I think David Beckham is probably the clearest example of this. The nation's tabloid press was shocked when he gave fans a single-fingered salute, but they neglected to mention the fact that these fans had been shouting at him for the previous ninety minutes, casting aspersions on his wife's sexual proclivities, and expressing their desire to see his baby son suffer serious illness. How can anyone be expected to put up with that? And Liverpool's Jamie Carragher received all kinds of sanctimonious strictures when he threw back into the crowd a coin that had been thrown at him. Footballers may be role models, but just as in society as a whole, people have rights and responsibilities. Forfeit one, and you lose the other. Abuse someone, and it's unlikely they'll turn the other cheek. Do as you would be done by, and all that, and don't pretend that you're shocked if a footballer swears at you after you've sworn at him. Footballers are human.

Rushden away

I would like to state here and now that I do not consider Rushden and Diamonds our local rivals. Indeed, it has taken a great degree of effort on my part to consider them a league club at all. It's an indictment on our recent decline that R&D is now our nearest away game. When we were in the old First Division, R&D didn't even exist. They were still two separate clubs, Irthlingborough Diamonds and Rushden Town, and only became the Rushden and Diamonds that we know now after multi-millionaire and owner of the Doctor Martens empire, Max Griggs, merged the two in an attempt to secure a place in the Football League.

Having said that, I acknowledge that R&D is a well run little club, with a nice enough stadium, and I have been reliably informed that lots of people from Bedford and its environs choose to go to Rushden now rather than Kenilworth Road. This concerns me a little, but at the end of the day I cannot conceive of Rushden being anything other than a non-league team. I'm sorry, Rushden fans, but it's true. I can't believe that today we are playing them in the league. This should never have happened.

I desperately want to thrash Rushden, just in an effort to put some distance between us and them. If we scored five or six, that would just prove that we are the mighty Luton Town, and Rushden have a bloody cheek even taking to the same pitch as us. In the end, we win 2-1, Howard and Crowe scoring, after two great crosses from Matty Taylor. Not exactly a comprehensive victory, but I do think the scoreline flatters Rushden a little. Still, three points is three points, and we've seen off another of the play off contenders. Which is another concern. How can Rushden be driving to get in Division Two? Surely they should be in the Conference?

March 12th 2002

Exeter home

The first home game I've missed all season, and the third overall. I guess it's not bad going. And like the other games I've missed, I do have a good reason.

Mr Fred Thomas, esteemed head of music at Queensbury School, Dunstable, former stalwart of Dunstable's Saturday Morning Music School, and leading light of several local amdram groups, is retiring this summer. He used to teach me, and he and his wife Pam have become friends of the family. So when he asked me to play bass in the pit orchestra for his last ever school show, West Side Story, I couldn't refuse. Indeed, I didn't want to. At the time Fred asked me if I was available, it was a blank week, and I could easily make the Tuesday night dress rehearsal and the four performances.

And then our New Year's Day game against Exeter was postponed. It was rearranged for three days later - and was postponed again. The next date convenient for both teams was March 12th. Dammit! What could I do? It wasn't like I didn't need the practice. West Side Story is a notoriously difficult score, and I hadn't touched a bass guitar for over two years. If I missed the one and only rehearsal, I certainly wouldn't be able to make it through the week without completely and dramatically ballsing it up - and I couldn't do that to Fred. So I donated my season ticket to my mum, on the proviso that she kept me informed with text messages throughout the game.

Apparently we won 3-0 without even breaking sweat. I get a lift to Luton station after the game, where Mark has waited for me in order to give me a full and detailed match report. It's a strange feeling, missing a home game. All evening, I felt uncomfortable; there was somewhere else I really should have been.

Kidderminster home

Ha. Jan Molby comes to Kenilworth Road. Before this season, I had no real feelings about Kidderminster (another non-league team, as far as I'm concerned), but now I despise them, and Molby, their own Big Fat Manager, after the whole postponement fiasco. Quite rightly, we thrashed them at Aggborough, and now we need to beat them at Castle Kenny, complete the double over them, and then they will never darken our door again.

We win 1-0, with a solitary Paul Hughes strike after quarter of an hour of the first half. We're probably good for about another couple of goals, but the three points are never really in doubt. Kidderminster's notoriously "dodgy keeper" Brock is sent off on sixty five minutes for using hands outside the penalty area, but we don't capitalise. And goalscorer Hughes is shown the red card in injury time for a second bookable offence. Although we may well miss him during his suspension, I'm confident now that the squad's strength in depth will be enough to see us through.

Our good run continues.

Halifax home

Now, on the other hand, I do like Halifax. Their chief executive was very friendly when we rang him up to ask if the kick off at the Shay could be delayed for ten minutes when we were stuck in traffic, so I really don't want them to get relegated. Unfortunately it does look as though they'll be returning to the Conference next season, and today, by putting five past them, we play a big part in condemning them to non-league football.

My dad's mate, Ade, comes with us. As a Spurs fan, he's not really used to witnessing performance of this magnitude of brilliance. With a five-nil win, we equal the all-time club record of consecutive victories in style. Spring and Coyne get one apiece in the first half, Howard, Crowe and Valois, showing his true ability, all score in the second. Halifax have a man sent off towards the end for an off-the-ball incident, but it makes no difference to the overall result. A wonderful display of imperious footballing ability. Three points against Swansea next week would guarantee our promotion.

March 28th, 2002

Transfer deadline day

There's a horrible feeling of foreboding. Matty Taylor, Matthew Spring and Emmy Boyce are all out of contract at the end of the season. It would be better for us to sell them today if we have to sell them at all, and not ride our luck with a tribunal in the summer. The most likely to go is Taylor; the Premiership scouts have apparently been sniffing round the boy salvaged by Luton as a seventeen year old after Oxford rejected him for being too fat. He himself is a Spurs fan, and indeed Tottenham are one of the clubs who have been linked with him. Joe has stated that he rates Taylor as worth two million pounds, and a possible future England international. He may well be talking his player up, but Taylor is young and has had an excellent season. He definitely has potential, even more so if someone could teach him how to defend.

In the end, no one goes. No one comes in, either, except Crystal Palace's Steve Kabba on loan, a forward whom Joe describes as "greased lightning". He's not expected to play a major part tomorrow, in the promotion decider, but will probably be on the bench.

Really, the most interesting thing about deadline day for me is that it's a year since we signed Steve Howard, and very few Luton fans knew who he was. How times change. Happy Howie Day, everyone.

March 30th, 2002

Promotion; Swansea away

The best day of my supporting life in a very long time.

It's Easter weekend. We've known all week that if we win today, then promotion is sealed and we will be back in Division Two next season. And if we win today, that makes ten consecutive victories - a new club record. Pretty damn impressive, if you think about it.

My dad's side of the family all live in South Wales, so we trek to Abertillery on Good Friday to stay with his cousin Mary, her husband Roger, and their two boys, Ryan and Liam. My dad, my sister, Liam and I set out for Swansea at half past eleven on Saturday morning - just a quick run down the M4, and we're there. The highlight of the journey is reading the illuminated signs on the bridges - "LUTON TOWN FANS TAKE JUNCTION 42". On arriving in Swansea, I'm half expecting the Mayor to be waiting for us to welcome us to his city, along with a town crier announcing to the citizens of Abertawe (that's Welsh for Swansea) that Big Fat Joe's Barmy Army are in town.

The Mayor's not there. We do however meet around 1200 other Luton fans (a good proportion of which, I am sad to say, I have not seen before this season. They all crawl out of the woodwork when we're successful. Where were you last season when we were shit?), and some rather unfriendly Swansea fans, who get less and less friendly as the game progresses.

I meet Mark and Kev on the terrace, along with Mark's flat-

124

mate, and John from my mailing list, who I've not met before today. I greet them all with a hug and a kiss, and a declaration, "We're going to get promoted today!" Although I am pretending to be confident, the problem with being a Luton fan is that you can never trust the team to fulfil their potential. We've been disappointed too many times in the past. I keep telling myself that this is a new era, this is Joe and Mick's team, this is an administration made up of fans, and things are different now. Somehow I never fully believe things until they happen.

As the first half wears on, I'm getting restless. Why haven't we scored yet? As soon as I voice my displeasure, Howie chases a through ball, takes it round the keeper to the byline yet manages to keep it in play, and puts in a beautiful cross for Matty Taylor to head down for our first goal. Just 45 minutes to hang on...and we're up.

The team runs out for the second half, minus Valois and Taylor (and Bayliss, who was subbed for Boycie in the first half because of what transpires to be a dislocated shoulder), but plus Forbesy and Peter Holmes. Holmes is famous for having gone to the FA School of Excellence in the same year as Michael Owen. He's one of Ricky Hill's signings, and hasn't really been given a run in the first team. He is however still young (I say "young", I mean "my age") and as he's getting more experience he's also getting a bit bigger and stronger, which makes it more likely he'll be able to establish himself in the squad. Kev comments to me how good it would be if Holmesy scored the goal that ensured our promotion.

And what a cracker it is! We cavort round the terraces, this must be it now, ten in a row, and promotion in the bag. Now we want Howie to score, to take his total to 18 for the season. He obliges, a powerful long-range drive taken brilliantly, and we're coasting. We on the terraces begin to sing each player's name in turn, as the game continues, and the players give us a wave or a thumbs-up sign. We let in a soft goal towards the end, and it's heartening to see how furious the players are at their failure to keep a clean sheet.

Final whistle.

We're up!

Words can't really express the emotion radiating around the ground. If your team have ever been promoted, you'll understand, I'm sure. I feel exhausted, as if I have been out on the pitch for the last eight months, kicking every ball with them. The stupidly early starts, the hours of travelling, the miles of traffic, the price of train fares, the ramshackle grounds, the heavy handed policing and stewarding....it doesn't matter any more. It's all been worth it.

The players run over to us, and I rush to the front with my

The London Gang celebrate promotion at Swansea,
That's Kev on the left and Mark on the right

camera. Insanely, the stewards and police begin to usher the players off the pitch. No one can believe it, least of all Nico, who is very angry at being made to leave. Yet none of us exit the ground. We stand there, and begin to chant, "WE WANT JOE", over and over again. The pleading tannoy announcements for us to leave are repeated - apparently the police have advised the Luton players and staff to remain in the changing rooms - but it's so clearly not going to happen. Cherry, the club secretary, is in the main stand, and she is obviously as happy as we are. She waves to us, as her name is chanted too. Then she and Mike Watson-Challis make their way onto the pitch. How he must be feeling...it must be incredible to put money into the club you adore, and then see it pay so many dividends. Although we love and admire Joe and Mick, it has to be borne in mind that Mike Watson-Challis is the architect of this success. Without him, we would not have been able to attract a manager of Joe's calibre to the club.

Then Joe and Mick emerge, with all the players (led by Nico, of course, who is now wearing shorts and vest - which bears the legend, "NICO - MATCH VEST" scrawled in pen on the front). We go wild, as they run over to us, and Nico breaks open the champagne. The TV cameras and photographers swarm in, along with the representatives of Nationwide, the league's sponsors, and the players pose for pictures (including bloody Foti. I know he has scored one whole goal this season, but I'm infuriated to see him there swigging champagne that he has not earned. Am I being churlish?). It's wonderful to see the team spirit. The boys clearly like each other, as well as having a great respect for Joe and Mick, and it makes me want to cry because I'm just so happy. Joe is hoisted aloft on the shoulders of Mick and Aaron Skelton (whose arm promptly breaks and falls off. No, I'm only joking).

After about half an hour of this party, the Swansea stewards and police are beginning to tire. It's only fair that we should allow them to go home. We, after all, have only just started our celebrations. We have four games left, and each and every one of them will be a carnival.

Mansfield home

We owe Mansfield a thrashing. They turned us over at their place, when we really didn't perform, and might as well not have been there. More significantly for me, Howie is now poised on 18 league goals, one behind the notorious Greenacre (whose name as far as my sister and I are concerned is now a byword for something that was reasonably good and interesting to start with, but suffered from over-exposure and now we are SICK of hearing it. Other items to fit into this category would be Dancing in the Moonlight by Toploader, and Kylie's now very boring hit Can't Get You Out Of My Head). It would be incredibly poetic justice if Howie were to overtake Greenacre today. A hat trick would do nicely.

Greenacre doesn't even start the game - boring boring Mansfield. I was looking forward to booing the greedy git. He comes on midway through the first half, when it becomes obvious that we are going to run riot. By half time we're 4-2 up. With Pezza and Bayls both out injured, Boycie returns at right back, with Marvin moving to the centre, and we look decidedly shaky in defence. How lucky we are, then, that we can score goals. Valois opens the scoring on 12 minutes, and Mansfield respond immediately from a Taylor error. Crowie puts us ahead again, Nico adds a penalty, and Howie gets the fourth. Mansfield pull one back, a nicely placed lob over Embo's head.

Howie gets his second of the game a few minutes after the restart, and we all go mad. Where are all the doubters who told me that Howie would never get 20 goals in a season? They are all sitting at the back singing, "One Stevie Howard", that's where they are. Ha. Inevitably, Greenacre does get a goal, but not before he's missed a sitter by whacking the ball against the post, and we all laugh and cheer ironically. Apparently the commentators on the local BBC radio station are disapproving of our haranguing of Greenacre. Tough. For my part, it's not just because he demanded so much money to join us, it's because I see him as the representative of all those who called for Howie to be sold and replaced with Greenacre, who they reckoned was a class above Howie. Those calls have been silenced now. Greenacre and Howie have got twenty goals apiece. One of them wants to play for Luton Town FC, one of them doesn't. One is a big strong target man working alongside a smaller goalpoacher, one is the small goalpoacher himself. They are not interchangeable players, and even if they were I'd still rather have Howie in my team for his pure strength of character. How anyone can argue otherwise is beyond me.

5-3 it finishes, and the team return to the pitch for a lap of honour. Nico is going mad with excitement, and steals our mascot Happy Harry's head in order to put it on himself, dance around the pitch for a bit then throw it into the crowd. I get to the front of the Kenny End, and shake hands with Big Mick, but sadly I still fail to get one of the players' shirts.

129

Valois in jail?

I am sitting at the computer in my parents' house, typing my coursework essays, with the TV on in the background. Anglia News begins.

WHAT? JEAN-LOUIS VALOIS ARRESTED? I read snippets of rumours on the message board earlier, but I thought they were wind-ups. It transpires that M Valois drank a little bit too much last night when celebrating with the squad, and was refused entry to Liquid, a dive of a nightclub in Luton town centre. A scuffle ensued, and Jean-Louis was arrested and kept at the police station overnight (I'm guessing that this was because he was too drunk to answer any questions). The newsreader also informs us that further arrests are expected to be made.

Oh, how proud I am to be a Luton fan. Why do boys have to ruin everything? In the end, all is well - he is let off with a caution, and promptly apologises to Joe. We're all now in our element trying to devise suitable songs to hail our French wizard with on Saturday - the favourite is "Jean Louis Valois, hits bouncers in the bar...." Poetry, no?

Feeder clubs

It all starts so innocently. A Dunstable-based Spurs fan comes on our message board to congratulate us on our promotion, and to make subtle enquiries about Matty Taylor. Unfortunately, he also makes a comment about how he's looking forward to the day when the link between our club and his is made official, when we become their feeder club. This is a sort of "big brother, little brother" idea - the junior partner would give the senior's youth squad players some first team experience, and the senior partner would take the junior's most promising young players; in return the "little brother's" financial security would be assured.

All hell breaks loose. Every Luton fan is adamant that this will never happen, and the Spurs fan seems genuinely mystified as to why we have such strong objections. After all, he asserts, Luton are only a small club, our gates suffer from our proximity to London, and we already have several common links with Tottenham - their Director of Football, David Pleat, was Luton boss on two separate occasions, they signed Gary Doherty from us, we get useful young players like Ian Hillier and previously Rory Allen from them. Why not make it official?

We'll tell you why not. Because one day in the near future, we won't be a small club any more. We'll be back in the First Division, pushing for promotion, and Spurs, on their current form,

131

may well be struggling against relegation. Only fifteen years ago, we were in the same (top) division as them, taking them and all the other "big" clubs on and beating them, and we will not accept that the current situation is irreversible. Every football team should be independent, running themselves without outside interference from other clubs who purport to be superior. As far as I'm concerned, the whole concept of "feeder clubs" is alien to football and sport in general.

Hull away

Our superstitions are at ridiculous levels now. I won't wear my trainers to football any more because I wore them to Rochdale when we lost. My dad insists on taking his big thick thermal gloves to every game; apparently it doesn't matter if he wears them, it's their presence at the ground that makes the difference. This morning, before we set off from my parents' house, we have a long and involved discussion about whether or not he should take his scarf to hang out of the car window. We conclude that, as the scarf has not been in attendance so far this season, it would be foolhardy and irresponsible of us to take it today. My sister, who misses most away games as she has to work on a Saturday morning, stands at the window with a totally bemused expression on her face as she watches us debate the matter.

But these things are important. It's not only the fans who have their lucky charms, players themselves are notoriously superstitious. Marvin Johnson, despite having been injured for much of the season (and, bless him, even when he is fit he's getting on a bit so can't frequently complete a game), has been a vital component of our promotion campaign. Apart from the fact that he's our club captain and senior pro (over fifteen years' loyal service now), he has hit on the secret of our success. No, it's not his tactical nous that's helped. It is in fact his insanely fluorescent hat and gloves, which he has been wearing in the warm ups and while he's on the bench for around four months now. As the weather is warming up, Marv is looking more and more silly. However, he doesn't care, and nor do we, because it seems that the hat and gloves are the key to our glorious season.

And today is indeed a glorious day. More sunshine beaming down on an open terrace, where we're sheltered from the biting wind that we noticed as soon as we stepped out of the car in Hull. I take up my usual position to the left of the goal, along with my dad, Graham and Mark, and we're soon joined by a lad from Kent, whom we met in Swansea last week. We also see Neil, the fella who sits next to us at Kenilworth Road, as well as Danny and Elsie, and my old schoolmate Dellar; and of course there are all the other familiar faces - I know few of their names but all of their faces. In all, there are 1700 Luton fans here today. That's marvellous when you think about it, because for us it's a pretty much meaningless game. Promotion is guaranteed, and we're just here for a party.

Hull were pre-season favourites for promotion. They've had vast financial backing; some git of a Hull fan came on our message board yesterday and declared Steve Howard (who cost £50,000) to be "a plank", and Gary Alexander, their own 20 goal striker who cost half a million, to be far superior. This puzzles me. This kind of statement is endemic among Luton fans too - the idea that a cheap player can't be any good. Of course, with Luton fans, they'd moan soon enough if we bought an expensive player who was good to average (witness the case of Mark Ovendale, a good Nationwide keeper but probably not worth the £425k that Ricky Hill shelled out on him).

But I digress. Pre-season, Hull also had a shrewd manager in Brian Little. Yet he has been sacked and replaced this week by our old friend Jan Molby, the Danish Scouser. In his honour, for this his first home game as boss of the Tigers, the terrace opposite us unfurl a huge Danish flag, which causes us great amusement. It's not as funny as the tannoy announcement before the game, though:

"Good afternoon, East Stand!" - huge cheers from the terrace to our left.

"Good afternoon, South Stand!" - huge cheers from the terrace facing us.

"Good afternoon, West Stand!" - huge cheers from the terrace to our right.

"Luton - THIS IS BOOTHFERRY PARK!" - great laughter from the Hatters hordes. Do we look intimidated? I don't think we do. We've won our last eleven games, we're already promoted, we've scored ninety goals this season. Our confidence will not be shaken by people telling ŭs where we are.

First half is a footballing lesson to Hull. We notch our first, a majestic header from an unmarked Howie, after 23 minutes. The second comes about five minutes before half time, after good work from Dean Crowe. This is a strange goal as we don't start celebrating until after the players do - Boothferry Park has a hill in the middle of the pitch, and the goal at the other end is on the other side of the slope. Therefore we don't see Crowie go round the keeper and defender and toe poke the ball in. Still, as soon as Crowie takes his shirt off and waves it round his head whilst galloping along the touchline, we guess that we've scored and cheer resoundingly.

In the second half, we take our foot off the pedal. It's a metaphorical cry of "Come and have a go if you think you're hard enough" to Hull - we invite them to give us their best shot and show us what they can do. Accordingly, Hull have the majority of possession, but do nothing with it. Embo makes a couple of saves, but none of Hull's attempts are particularly worrying for us. In the last ten minutes, we decide to emphasise our excellence - Howie notches his second of the game with around eight minutes to go, and has another couple of close shaves. Howie has scored two on several occasions this season, but has never scored three in a game in his entire career. My dad and Graham shake their heads like wise old men and say, "Poor Howie, he's destined never to get a hat trick, certainly not this season, anyway." I castigate the doubters, and tell them, "Yes, he will, he'll do it today."

With one minute left, we launch our final attack. And then...and then...Howie is in the box, directly in front of us. He has a man marking him, and the keeper to beat. He shrugs off his marker, closes in on the keeper, angle becoming ever more acute...goes round the keeper....shoots...it's IN!!!!!!!!

I have literally not been so happy for years. I am screaming, I am jumping up and down, my eyes are misting up. Howie comes over to our section of the terrace and is mobbed by his ecstatic team mates. Nico in particular seems to have gone mad, again, strangely; he clenches his fist, yells "AAAAAAAAAAAAAAAAH!" and then kicks an advertising hoarding, probably because he is frustrated at the stewards ushering them all back from us, both after this goal and after the final whistle. It's sad to say, but apparently there was a bit of trouble in one of the pubs before the game. This is why we all get kept in the ground for twenty minutes after the end of the match until the surrounding streets have been cleared. Yet if we hadn't been kept in, I wouldn't have witnessed one of the most touching displays of appreciation ever - the Hull fans, as they head towards the exit nearest our terrace, begin to applaud us. Genuine recognition, I would think, of a great army of travelling fans, and a great team who totally outclassed their own. We clap them back. It's nice to see that opposing fans don't necessarily have to fight each other.

The players do their traditional applauding of the fans as well. Howie has a huge grin on his face and the match ball up his shirt. His team mates are all patting him on the back and hugging him. The team spirit, again, is a delight to behold. They are all rightly proud of him and each other. Howie is top scorer in Division Three now, notching 23 goals in the league, and as a team we've got 94 goals. We have two games left to score six more and break the magic hundred league goals barrier. On this form, it looks like we may well do it.

A wonderful day is topped off when the tannoy man announces the full time scores from around the country. Southend have held Plymouth to a goalless draw, and we top the table on goal difference. Today has been one of the best days in my years of supporting Luton. I may be poor because I can't work at weekends, I may not have done any of my coursework today, I may not have a boyfriend because I spend all my time travelling round the country to watch the lads - but days like this make it all worthwhile.

April 9th, 2002

Just a girl

I haven't really dwelt on the fact that I'm a girl who spends the majority of her leisure time in what has traditionally been and essentially still is a man's world, but of course I am and I do. I don't think that my gender makes a lot of difference. Certainly my bloke friends don't treat me any differently; if they started to patronise me they know they'd probably get thumped. I've been a football fan since childhood, and I like to think that my all-round knowledge of the game is equal to that of most men's. Very occasionally I do get some sad man challenging me to a trivia quiz, which I invariably win, and I have no problems with him from there on in. I do have to say though that I think my being a woman has helped to settle the nerves of certain players when I've interviewed them, but even then they haven't talked down to me; they've all accepted me as a fan and a journalist who knows what she's talking about, for which I'm very grateful.

So today is quite an exception. On reading some of the archived posts to my mailing list, I find one sent in September; like most of the mails sent around that time it was an attack on Steve Howard. This was also an attack on me though. Its writer declared that the reason that I was the only one defending Howie was because of my gender and my inherent incomprehension of the game, and any normal football fan (implying "any man") wanted Howard sacked immediately because he would prove to be of no use. Women, he went on to say, have no place in football.

Of course, I've gone on to be proved right. So I decide to forward this old mail to the list, and enquire whether its author would now like to apologise to me. He grudgingly admits that I was correct about Steve Howard and his ability, as well as about Aaron Skelton and his fitness level. Yet he stands by his opinion that women should not be involved in the Beautiful Game.

I am really shocked by this. My judgement of players has been demonstrably spot-on in its accuracy - and yet a man who seems to have no ability when recognising a good or a bad player thinks that he has more right to be at a game than me? I don't understand. I know there are some women who call themselves football fans, but only occasionally watch a game, and even when they do can't comprehend what's happening. But I'm not one of these. And equally, there are men who have to rely on their more informed friends to tell them what's going on, but still think they have a right to pass opinion purely because of their Y-chromosome. It's distressing that some men in the twenty-first century still hold such outdated views.

PFA Division Three Team of the Year

Today, the penultimate Friday of the season, the PFA Division Three Team of the Year is announced. This is a supposedly democratic vote, decided by each member of the players' union. Luton Town, top of the league, with 94 goals scored so far, on a winning run of twelve consecutive games, have only one representative in the team, that being Matty Taylor.

I am gobsmacked. How can the teams that we've torn apart this season not recognise our players? I cannot think of a better central defensive partnership in the division than Russ Perrett and Chris Coyne. Steve Howard is the league's top goalscorer. The classy Jean Louis Valois knows more tricks than some of these teams put together. In fact, man for man, I would not replace any of our first team with any other player in Division Three. That is how good we are now.

Someone sensibly points out that the voting for the Team of the Year occurs during January and February, when we were on a poor run, losing three out of four games. Even so, for me there has only been one single opposing player that has stood out as exceptionally good, and that's Peter Beagrie. Chris Greenacre was decent enough at Field Mill, but dreadful at Kenilworth Road. I missed the Plymouth away game, but none of them shone when we played them at home. As for the rest of them...words fail me.

Joe Kinnear has many faults, but being lost for words is not one of them. He declares that he is now intending to boycott the PFA's black-tie dinner, scheduled for Sunday, in protest. He is outraged. It's nice to know we have a manager who cares.

Macclesfield home

The club have declared today "Hatters Day". It's our last home game of the season, and fans are requested to come to the ground wearing some form of head gear.

I must state here and now that I am a hat person. I decide that I must do something special to celebrate this glorious season, but inspiration seems to be lacking. Then I hit on it. I must create a tribute to Kevin Nicholls. I perform a pastiche on his now-infamous scrawl - NICO - MATCH VEST. Digging out my old pink straw hat, complete with navy blue band, I sew on letters made of orange felt, which proclaim - CARRIE - MATCH HAT. Adding some swirls of orange, navy and white ribbons, my hat is a work of art inspired by comedy genius. I am proud.

It also gives me great pride to read in the match day programme that the club's guests of honour today are the families of Les Sealey and Marc North - the two former players who sadly passed away this season. I hope it gives them some comfort to know that the club and the fans will not forget Les or Marc's service to Luton Town.

I am less proud of today's display. Gunning for thirteen wins in a row, and another three points in order to stay top of the table, we stutter to a halt and a poor nil-nil draw against a defensive Macclesfield side. The highlight of it is when Matty Taylor goes down after a clash of heads, and Nico screams at him to stop messing about, get back on his feet and play on. Brilliant.

The squad and officials return to the pitch for another lap of honour after the game, but it's muted. It's nice to see the players bring their children with them. Aussie Chris Coyne is cradling his four-month-old baby, Kieran (whom my sister continually refers to as "Dingo", because "it's an Australian name"), Adrian Forbes' boy, Jordan, is running about all over the place (he's obviously inherited his daddy's speed), and Nico, of course, carries out his little girl, Kaylea, sporting a Luton top with DADDY printed on the back (and not, to my surprise, NICO - MATCH BABY). Marv's two children are a lot older than these other kids, showing just how big the age gap is between him and the rest of the squad. Matty Taylor is in his element with the kids, and we speculate on whether the daddies permit young Matty to babysit for them. Much as we try to entertain ourselves, there's no disguising the fact that it's a total anti-climax.

Despondently, Mark, Kev, Kev's brother and I trudge to the Wellington, where we have a few drinks and learn that Plymouth won, and so did Watford. Days don't really get any worse.

We go on to Balti Nights for a curry, where I am greeted with the cry, "Hatters lady!" Maybe I go for too many curries and to too many football games? Naaaaah.

April 15th, 2002

No one likes us

Plymouth beat Darlington 4-1 tonight, and in doing so secure the Third Division Championship. Instead of going out and celebrating, as you'd expect fans of title-winning teams to do, a section of their fans decide to connect to the internet, log onto Luton messageboards and gloat.

All season, there's been rivalry between us and Plymouth, triggered mainly by an inept Devonian journalist who didn't understand the concept of comments being tongue-in-cheek, and reported Joe's mickey-taking speeches as serious. Joe's latest outbursts regarding the PFA Division Three Team of the Year seem to have been the final straw. Supporters of Plymouth, Mansfield and of course Watford are invading our websites and telling us that we're the most hated club in the Nationwide League.

Most hated club? Well, there's an accolade. I suspect that much of this hatred is borne of jealousy. Joe is the kind of manager adored by his own fans, simply because he's inclined to talk up his players to the detriment of the opposition. Naturally, this riles opponents. But I think that any of these people who profess to hate Luton Town and Joe Kinnear would be more than pleased should Joe be appointed manager at their club. I'm certainly glad that he's on our side and not against us.

And now, with our outspoken manager co-ordinating matters on the pitch admirably, we have big plans. The long-mooted brand new 15,000 seater stadium looks close to being a reality now that the wonderful Mike Watson-Challis has bought the land adjacent to Junction 10 of the M1. His money enables us to attract good quality players to Kenilworth Road - resulting in the first instance in this season's promotion and record breaking run. Although Plymouth are certainly more consistent than us and deserve this season's championship, there's no doubt that we are the more exciting team to watch. I know that no one remembers who comes second, but the Third Division title isn't really all that important; I honestly think I would rather have watched a team produce episodes of scintillating football, than have watched a team grind out single goal wins all season. That's totally contrary to what I have always believed. I've continually maintained that I would be happier seeing Luton playing Route One football, fluking a season of one-nil wins and winning trophies, instead of seeing them playing the pretty passing game, winning half our games magnificently and finishing second. Yet this season has been so much fun, I'm not sure I'd change any of it. Yes, of course it would have been nice to get the title, but the ups and downs of this year have made it what it is - the most exciting season that I can remember. For instance, our twelve-in-a-row wouldn't have been so special if we hadn't lost three out of the four previous games, and Howie's 23 goals (so far) wouldn't have been so fantastic if he hadn't gone through the York episode.

So we're second. Who cares? We're still up. And Joe - don't worry about what other people say, because we love you!

Shrewsbury away

The end of the road. Almost a year to the day we were relegated from Division Two, we play our final game in Division Three. It's a full car on the way up - as well as me, my dad, Graham and Mark, my sister joins us, having taken the day off work to celebrate promotion. She joins in with the singalong on the way up; we give fantastic renditions of the same songs that we've played for every away game during this unbeaten run (Harvest for the World, September, Best of my Love, The One and Only, Can't Take My Eyes off You, Run for Home, You're So Vain...to name but a few).

From the outset, today is not as good as it could be. This is because I am in pain, after having two teeth out as the precursor to planned orthodontic work. When we arrive in Shrewsbury, we go to a takeaway, and I have great problems trying to eat a burger. It's pitiful. To add insult to injury, all the pubs in the town centre have been closed. So we head straight to the away terrace.

Kevin Nicholls isn't playing today. He's being rested, because if he picks up another booking he'll be suspended for the start of next season. And instead of sitting in the stand with the club officials, he, along with Lee Mansell and the injured Peter Holmes, joins us on the terrace, while the recuperating Dave Bayliss joins the Luton fans in the seats to the side. I say hello to Nico briefly, and get a photo taken with all three players (although I am told that this is "a bit girly" of me. It seems to have escaped their notice that I am actually a girl. Oh well). Everyone really appreciates this gesture from the players; how many other clubs would have squad members mingling with fans at a match? Nico is really wound up, and leads the singing, starting with a serenade of Jean Louis Valois (and then, bizarrely, he begins a chorus of "One Kevin Nicholls". Funny boy). One fan presents Nico with a cone shaped thing, which makes a hooting noise when you blow it. He seems delighted with his new toy, and screams at JLV to run the length of the pitch and come and talk to him. The conversation is minimal: "Here you are, Jean, have a blow on my hooter," says Nico, to which Jean Louis giggles, and replies, "Non, non!" Undeterred, Nico calls and waves to all his team mates, who grin and wave back.

Shrewsbury need to get a result today in order to get a play off place. Ostensibly, we're playing for nothing but pride. However, there's a minor issue at stake - the Division Three Golden Boot. Shrewsbury striker Luke Rodgers is one goal behind our very own Steve Howard (or "Steven Howard" as the official League goalscorers' chart refers to him) in the goalscoring stakes. Rodgers is the only real challenge to Howie, unless Greenacre manages to notch a hat trick for Mansfield today (although as he's only scored half a dozen goals since December, it's quite unlikely). I say as much to my dad, and he is shocked that I have even voiced such a sacrilegious opinion. He tells me, quite seriously, "Rodgers won't score. Russ and Chris won't let that happen," referring of course to our magnificent centre halves Perrett and Coyne.

It's another poor game, not helped by the referee appearing to think that we've all come to see him blow his whistle every thirty seconds. Shrewsbury have quite a bit of possession but never look like doing anything with it; Rodgers is sharp and quick, but not the predatory striker I was expecting to see. Just before half time, Howie races down the left wing, puts in a cross, which bounces into the net off the boot of Shrews full back Greg Rioch, under pressure from Dean Crowe. Ironically, this is the first own goal for us all season, and it's scored by a former Luton trainee, who's also the son of Hatters legend Bruce Rioch. Howie tries to claim it, his reasoning being that he was the last Luton player to touch the ball, as does Crowie, because he's on a bonus if he scores more than fifteen goals - but it's definitely an own goal.

The second half is much the same. Towards the end, we are entertained by a streaker (male) who leaps out from the home terrace, gallops across the pitch, and is not accosted by anyone. Stewards, police and players stand there and watch him, not making any attempt to stop him. He doesn't know what to do without anyone chasing him, and eventually jumps back into the terrace...and is promptly arrested.

Ninety minutes on the clock, and the fourth official holds up the board, which proclaims that there will be seven minutes of injury time.

Therein lies more irony. The last time that we played a game when there was seven minutes added on was at Bootham Crescent - York away, 15th September 2001 - the day that Howie missed those two penalties and was nearly hounded out of the club. (The time added on that day was for the same reason as today - Luton fans trying to waste time by holding onto the ball when it went out of play.) Six minutes into added time, the ball is squared across the box by Taylor. It falls to Howie, two yards out at the far post. He tucks it away with aplomb, sealing the victory and his own Golden Boot.

At the final whistle, the team do yet another lap of honour. Thank you to the staff and fans of Shrewsbury Town, who stay to applaud us, and who put a message across the tannoy wishing us luck for next season. It's Mansfield who will be joining us in the Second as the third club promoted from Division Three, as they pip Cheltenham to the final automatic promotion spot.

So that's it. Joe Kinnear, Mick Harford, Brian Stein and John Moore have turned the playing fortunes of Luton Town FC around in less than a year. Mike Watson Challis and his board of directors, supported by the hard working club secretary Cherry Newbery, have put the club on a sound financial footing. And of course the players have performed admirably - some of whom were in our relegated team last year, but most of which were brought in by Joe over the summer, and have proved themselves to be dedicated, hard working professionals, with a true respect for their Gaffer and the fans who pay their wages.

This is the best season that I can remember. When Danny Clubb, the Blackpool Hatter, told me back in December that it's much more special seeing your team win promotion than it is seeing them win a one-off cup competition, I didn't understand him. Being twenty-two, I don't remember our last promotion season; I've seen the Littlewoods Cup win, and several other cup runs, but league-wise all I can recall is fighting for survival, then successive relegations. Now I know. Gaining ninety-seven points over the course of a season is a phenomenal achievement; we have broken the hundred goal barrier if you include our cup goals as well. Thirteen wins and one draw out of our last fourteen games; fifteen away wins (and fifteen home wins) in total is an unbelievable record. We may not be consistent, but it's definitely very exciting to watch. It's a wonderful time to be a Luton fan. The good times are back.

So again - thank you to the players and staff of Luton Town FC for making 2001-2002 a year to remember. It's only one hundred and twelve days until the beginning of next season.

APPENDIX A

LUTON TOWN FC – RESULTS 2001/2002

August 11th, 2001	Carlisle United (a)	0-2	Hughes 46, Griffiths 57	4,432
August 18th, 2001	Cheltenham Town (h)	2-1	Hughes 30, Griffiths 37	6,177
August 21st, 2002	Reading (a) – Worthington Cup	0-4		5,115
August 25th, 2001	Bristol Rovers (a)	3-2	Taylor 42, Mansell 81	9,057
August 27th, 2001	Southend United (h)	2-0	Griffiths 80, Fotiadis 83	6,496
September 1st, 2001	Exeter City (a)	2-2	Taylor 35, 52	3,088
September 8th, 2001	Oxford United (h)	1-1	Nicholls 9	6,736
September 15th, 2001	York City (a)	1-2	Griffiths 41, Hillier 74	3,247
September 18th, 2001	Lincoln City (h)	1-1	Skelton 8	5,066
September 22nd, 2001	Torquay United (h)	5-1	Howard 18, Griffiths 31, 47, 78, Valois 60	6,392
September 25th, 2001	Leyton Orient (a)	1-3	Taylor 30, Valois 53, Howard 67	6,540
September 29th, 2001	Plymouth Argyle (a)	2-1	Crowe 15	5,782
October 5th, 2001	Darlington (h)	5-2	Spring 35, Howard 47, Crowe 67, Nicholls 72 (pen), Valois 82	7,219
October 13th, 2001	Scunthorpe (a)	2-0	Forbes 65, Perrett 72	3,939
October 20th, 2001	Rochdale (h)	0-1		7,696
October 23rd, 2001	Halifax Town (a)	2-4	Crowe 31, 45, Nicholls 86 Forbes 88	2,140
October 27th, 2001	Swansea City (h)	3-0	Crowe 23, Perrett 54, Forbes 61	6,705
October 30th, 2001	Dagenham & Redbridge (a) – LDV Round 2	2-3	Mansell 56, Thomson 67	2,433
November 3rd, 2001	Mansfield Town (a)	4-1	Crowe 85	5,973
November 9th, 2001	Shrewsbury Town (h)	1-0	Spring 71	6,809
November 17th, 2001	Southend United (a) – FA Cup Round 1	3-2	Forbes 34, Brkovic 75	6,526
November 20th, 2001	Hull City (h)	0-1		7,214
November 24th, 2001	Macclesfield Town (a)	4-1	Howard 32	2,250
December 8th, 2001	Hartlepool United (a)	1-2	Crowe 30, Taylor 45	3,585
December 15th, 2001	Rushden and Diamonds (h)	1-0	Crowe 34	7,495
December 22nd, 2001	Hartlepool United (h)	2-2	Howard 35, Johnson 84	6,739
December 26th, 2001	Oxford United (a)	1-2	Crowe 39, Spring 46	11,121

December 29th, 2001	Southend United (a)	1-2	Crowe 67, Taylor 83	5,973
January 8th, 2002	Kidderminster Harriers (a)	1-4	Taylor 53, Spring 55, 69, Howard 58	4,147
January 12th, 2002	Cheltenham Town (a)	1-1	Howard 73	5,026
January 19th, 2002	Carlisle United (h)	1-1	Perrett 67	6,647
January 26th, 2002	Darlington (a)	3-2	Howard 12, Valois 60	3,560
February 2nd, 2002	Plymouth (h)	2-0	Nicholls 79 (pen), Howard 86	9,585
February 9th, 2002	Rochdale (a)	1-0		4,306
February 16th, 2002	Scunthorpe United (h)	2-3	Howard 35, Taylor 77	6,371
February 19th, 2002	Bristol Rovers (h)	3-0	Howard 47, Coyne 65, Nicholls 76 (pen)	5,651
February 23rd, 2002	York City (h)	2-1	Howard 18, 50	6,188
February 26th, 2002	Lincoln City (a)	0-1	Taylor 41	2,921
March 2nd, 2002	Torquay United (a)	0-1	Brkovic 20	3,280
March 5th, 2002	Leyton Orient (h)	3-0	Coyne 36, Crowe 48, Forbes 66	6,683
March 9th, 2002	Rushden and Diamonds (a)	1-2	Crowe 58, Howard 81	5,876
March 12th, 2002	Exeter City (h)	3-0	Howard 26, 64, Taylor 78	6,327
March 16th, 2002	Kidderminster Harriers (h)	1-0	Hughes 16	6,488
March 23rd, 2002	Halifax Town (h)	5-0	Spring 20, Coyne 32, Howard 49, Crowe 75, Valois 87	6,830
March 30th, 2002	Swansea City (a)	1-3	Taylor 31, Holmes 58, Howard 78	5,436
April 1st, 2002	Mansfield Town (h)	5-3	Valois 11, Crowe 22, Nicholls 30 (pen), Howard 34, 49	8,231
April 6th, 2002	Hull City (a)	0-4	Howard 23, 79, 89, Crowe 38	9,379
April 13th, 2002	Macclesfield Town (h)	0-0		7,873
April 20th, 2002	Shrewsbury Town (a)	0-2	Rioch (og) 36, Howard 90	7,858

APPENDIX B

DIVISION THREE 2001/2002 - LEADING SCORERS
(not including play-offs)

Steve Howard	Luton Town	24
Luke Rodgers	Shrewsbury Town	22
Chris Greenacre	Mansfield Town	21
Julian Alsop	Cheltenham Town	20
Onandi Lowe	Rushden and Diamonds	19
Gordon Watson	Hartlepool United	18
Gary Alexander	Hull City	17
Dean Crowe	**Luton Town**	**15**
Richie Foran	Carlisle United	14
Michael Proctor	York City	14
Kevin Townson	Rochdale	14
Martin Carruthers	Scunthorpe United	13
Paul Moody	Oxford United	13
Lee Nogan	York City	13
Lee Thorpe	Lincoln City	13
Lawrie Dudfield	Hull City	12
Tony Naylor	Cheltenham Town	12
Steve Torpey	Scunthorpe United	12
Peter Beagrie	Scunthorpe United	11
Graham Coughlan	Plymouth Argyle	11
Paul Harsley	Halifax Town	11
Matthew Taylor	**Luton Town**	**11**
Jamie Brooks	Oxford United	10

APPENDIX C

DIVISION THREE 2001/2002 - FINAL TABLE

	P	W	D	L	F	A	W	D	L	F	A	GD	Pts
Plymouth Argyle	46	19	2	2	41	11	12	7	4	30	17	43	**102**
Luton Town	46	15	5	3	50	18	15	2	6	46	30	48	**97**
Mansfield Town	46	17	3	3	49	24	7	4	12	23	36	12	**79**
Cheltenham Town	46	11	11	1	40	20	10	4	9	26	29	17	**78**
Rochdale	46	13	8	2	41	22	8	7	8	24	30	13	**78**
Rushden &Diamonds	46	14	5	4	40	20	6	8	9	29	33	16	**73**
Hartlepool United	46	12	6	5	53	23	8	5	10	21	25	26	**71**
Scunthorpe United	46	14	5	4	43	22	5	9	9	31	34	18	**71**
Shrewsbury Town	46	13	4	6	36	19	7	6	10	28	34	11	**70**
Kidderminster Harriers	46	13	6	4	35	17	6	3	14	21	30	9	**66**
Hull City	46	12	6	5	38	18	4	7	12	19	33	6	**61**
Southend United	46	12	5	6	36	22	3	8	12	15	32	-3	**58**
Macclesfield Town	46	7	7	9	23	25	8	6	9	18	27	-11	**58**
York City	46	11	5	7	26	20	5	4	14	28	47	-13	**57**
Darlington	46	11	6	6	37	25	4	5	14	23	46	-11	**56**
Exeter City	46	7	9	7	25	32	7	4	12	23	41	-25	**55**
Carlisle United	46	11	5	7	31	21	1	11	11	18	35	-7	**52**
Leyton Orient	46	10	7	6	37	25	3	6	14	18	46	-16	**52**
Torquay United	46	8	6	9	27	31	4	9	10	19	32	-17	**51**
Swansea City	46	7	8	8	26	26	6	4	13	27	51	-24	**51**
Oxford United	46	8	7	8	34	28	3	7	13	19	34	-9	**47**
Lincoln City	46	8	4	11	25	27	2	12	9	19	35	-18	**46**
Bristol Rovers	46	8	7	8	28	28	3	5	15	12	32	-20	**45**
Halifax Town	46	5	9	9	24	28	3	3	17	15	56	-45	**36**

Books Published by THE BOOK CASTLE

COUNTRYSIDE CYCLING IN BEDFORDSHIRE, BUCKINGHAMSHIRE AND
HERTFORDSHIRE: Mick Payne. Twenty rides on and off-road for all the family.
PUB WALKS FROM COUNTRY STATIONS: Bedfordshire and Hertfordshire: Clive Higgs.
Fourteen circular country rambles, each starting and finishing at a railway station and
incorporating a pub stop at a mid way point.
PUB WALKS FROM COUNTRY STATIONS: Buckinghamshire and Oxfordshire: Clive Higgs.
Circular rambles incorporating pub-stops.
LOCAL WALKS: South Bedfordshire and North Chilterns: Vaughan Basham.
Twenty-seven thematic circular walks.
LOCAL WALKS: North and Mid Bedfordshire: Vaughan Basham. Twenty-five thematic
circular walks.
FAMILY WALKS: Chilterns South: Nick Moon. Thirty 3 to 5 mile circular walks.
FAMILY WALKS: Chilterns North: Nick Moon. Thirty shorter circular walks.
CHILTERN WALKS: Hertfordshire, Bedfordshire and North Bucks: Nick Moon.
CHILTERN WALKS: Buckinghamshire: Nick Moon.
CHILTERN WALKS: Oxfordshire and West Buckinghamshire: Nick Moon.
A trilogy of circular walks, in association with the Chiltern Society. Each volume contains
30 circular walks.
OXFORDSHIRE WALKS: Oxford, the Cotswolds and the Cherwell Valley: Nick Moon.
OXFORDSHIRE WALKS: Oxford, the Downs and the Thames Valley: Nick Moon.
Two volumes that complement Chiltern Walks: Oxfordshire, and complete coverage of the county,
in association with the Oxford Fieldpaths Society. Thirty circular walks in each.
THE D'ARCY DALTON WAY: Nick Moon. Long-distance footpath across the Oxfordshire
Cotswolds and Thames Valley, with various circular walk suggestions.
THE CHILTERN WAY: Nick Moon. A guide to the new 133 mile circular Long-Distance Path
through Bedfordshire, Buckinghamshire, Hertfordshire and Oxfordshire, as planned by the Chiltern
Society.
CHANGES IN OUR LANDSCAPE: Aspects of Bedfordshire, Buckinghamshire and the Chilterns
1947-1992: Eric Meadows. Over 350 photographs from the author's collection
spanning nearly 50 years.
JOURNEYS INTO BEDFORDSHIRE: Anthony Mackay. Foreword by The Marquess of
Tavistock, Woburn Abbey. A lavish book of over 150 evocative ink drawings.
COCKNEY KID & COUNTRYMEN: Ted Enever. The Second World War remembered by the
children of Woburn Sands and Aspley Guise. A six year old boy is evacuated from London's East
End to start life in a Buckinghamshire village.
CHANGING FACES, CHANGING PLACES: Post war Bletchley and Woburn Sands
1945-1970 Ted Enever. Evocative memoirs of post-war life on the Beds/Bucks borders, up to the
coming of Milton Keynes new town.
BUCKINGHAM AT WAR: Pip Brimson. Stories of courage, humour and pathos as Buckingham
people adapt to war.
WINGS OVER WING: The Story of a World War II Bomber Training Unit: Mike Warth.
The activities of RAF Wing in Buckinghamshire.
JOURNEYS INTO BUCKINGHAMSHIRE: Anthony Mackay. Superb line drawings plus
background text: large format landscape gift book.

BUCKINGHAMSHIRE MURDERS: Len Woodley. Nearly two centuries of nasty crimes.

WINGRAVE: A Rothschild Village in the Vale: Margaret and Ken Morley. Thoroughly researched and copiously illustrated survey of the last 200 years in this lovely village between Aylesbury and Leighton Buzzard.

HISTORIC FIGURES IN THE BUCKINGHAMSHIRE LANDSCAPE: John Houghton. Major personalities and events that have shaped the county's past, including Bletchley Park.

TWICE UPON A TIME: John Houghton. North Bucks short stories loosely based on fact.

SANCTITY AND SCANDAL IN BEDS AND BUCKS: John Houghton. A miscellany of unholy people and events.

MANORS and MAYHEM, PAUPERS and PARSONS: Tales from Four Shires: Beds., Bucks., Herts. and Northants: John Houghton. Little known historical snippets and stories.

THE LAST PATROL: Policemen killed on duty while serving the Thames Valley: Len Woodley.

FOLK: Characters and Events in the History of Bedfordshire and Northamptonshire: Vivienne Evans. Anthology of people of yesteryear -arranged alphabetically by village or town.

JOHN BUNYAN: His Life and Times: Vivienne Evans. Highly praised and readable account.

THE RAILWAY AGE IN BEDFORDSHIRE: Fred Cockman. Classic, illustrated account of early railway history.

A LASTING IMPRESSION: Michael Dundrow. A boyhood evacuee recalls his years in the Chiltern village of Totternhoe near Dunstable.

ELEPHANTS I'LL NEVER FORGET: A Keeper's Life at Whipsnade and London Zoo: John Weatherhead. Experiences, dramatic and sad, from a lifetime with these well-loved giants.

WHIPSNADE MY AFRICA: Lucy Pendar. The inside story of sixty years of this world-renowned institution. Full of history, anecdotes, stories of animals and people.

GLEANINGS REVISITED: Nostalgic Thoughts of a Bedfordshire Farmer's Boy: E.W. O'Dell. His own sketches and early photographs adorn this lively account of rural Bedfordshire in days gone by.

BEDFORDSHIRE'S YESTERYEARS: The Rural Scene: Brenda Fraser-Newstead. Vivid first-hand accounts of country life two or three generations ago.

BEDFORDSHIRE'S YESTERYEARS: Craftsmen and Tradespeople: Brenda Fraser-Newstead. Fascinating recollections over several generations practising many vanishing crafts and trades.

BEDFORDSHIRE'S YESTERYEARS: War Times and Civil Matters: Brenda Fraser-Newstead. Two World Wars, plus transport, law and order, etc.

DUNNO'S ORIGINALS: A facsimile of the rare pre-Victorian history of Dunstable and surrounding villages. New preface and glossary by John Buckledee, Editor of The Dunstable Gazette.

DUNSTABLE DOWN THE AGES: Joan Schneider and Vivienne Evans. Succinct overview of the town's prehistory and history - suitable for all ages.

HISTORIC INNS OF DUNSTABLE: Vivienne Evans. Illustrated booklet, especially featuring ten pubs in the town centre.

EXPLORING HISTORY ALL AROUND: Vivienne Evans. Planned as seven circular car tours, plus background to places of interest en-route in Bedfordshire and parts of Bucks and Herts.

PROUD HERITAGE: A Brief History of Dunstable, 1000-2000AD: Vivienne Evans. Century by century account of the town's rich tradition and key events, many of national significance.

DUNSTABLE WITH THE PRIORY: 1100-1550: Vivienne Evans. Dramatic growth of Henry I's important new town around a major crossroads.

DUNSTABLE IN TRANSITION: 1550-1700: Vivienne Evans. Wealth of original material as the town evolves without the Priory.

DUNSTABLE DECADE: THE EIGHTIES: A Collection of Photographs: Pat Lovering. A souvenir book of nearly 300 pictures of people and events in the 1980's

STREETS AHEAD: An Illustrated Guide to the Origins of Dunstable's Street Names: Richard Walden. Fascinating text and captions to hundreds of photographs, past and present, throughout the town.

DUNSTABLE IN DETAIL: Nigel Benson. A hundred of the town's buildings and features, plus town trail map.

DUNSTAPLE: A Tale of The Watling Highway: A.W. Mooring. Dramatic novelisation of Dunstable's legend of Dunne the Robber - reprinted after a century out of print.

25 YEARS OF DUNSTABLE: Bruce Turvey. Reissue of this photographic treasure-trove of the town up to the Queen's Silver Jubilee, 1952-77.

DUNSTABLE SCHOOL: 1888-1971. F.M. Bancroft. Short history of one of the town's most influential institutions.

BOURNE and BRED: A Dunstable Boyhood Between the Wars: Colin Bourne. An elegantly written, well illustrated book capturing the spirit of the town over fifty years ago.

OLD HOUGHTON: Pat Lovering. Pictorial record capturing the changing appearances of Houghton Regis over the past 100 years.

ROYAL HOUGHTON: Pat Lovering. Illustrated history of Houghton Regis from the earliest of times to the present.

WERE YOU BEING SERVED?: Remembering 50 Luton Shops of Yesteryear: Bob Norman. Well-illustrated review of the much loved, specialist outlets of a generation or two ago.

GIRLS IN BLUE: Christine Turner. The activities of the famous Luton Girls Choir properly documented over its 41 year period from 1936 to 1977.

THE STOPSLEY BOOK: James Dyer. Definitive, detailed account of this historic area of Luton. 150 rare photographs.

THE STOPSLEY PICTURE BOOK: James Dyer. New material and photographs make an ideal companion to The Stopsley Book.

PUBS and PINTS: The Story of Luton's Public Houses and Breweries: Stuart Smith. The background to beer in the town, plus hundreds of photographs, old and new.

LUTON AT WAR - VOLUME ONE: As compiled by the Luton News in 1947, a well illustrated thematic account.

LUTON AT WAR - VOLUME TWO: Second part of the book compiled by The Luton News.

THE CHANGING FACE OF LUTON: An Illustrated History: Stephen Bunker, Robin Holgate and Marian Nichols. Luton's development from earliest times to the present busy industrial town. Illustrated in colour and mono.

WHERE THEY BURNT THE TOWN HALL DOWN: Luton, The First World War and the Peace Day Riots, July 1919: Dave Craddock. Detailed analysis of a notorious incident.

THE MEN WHO WORE STRAW HELMETS: Policing Luton, 1840-1974: Tom Madigan. Fine chronicled history, many rare photographs; author~served in Luton Police for fifty years.

BETWEEN THE HILLS: The Story of Lilley, a Chiltern Village: Roy Pinnock. A priceless piece of our heritage - the rural beauty remains but the customs and way of life described here have largely disappeared.

KENILWORTH SUNSET: A Luton Town Supporter's Journal: Tim Kingston. Frank and funny account of football's ups and downs.

A HATTER GOES MAD!: Kristina Howells. Luton Town footballers, officials and supporters talk to a female fan.
LEGACIES: Tales and Legends of Luton and the North Chilterns: Vic Lea. Mysteries and stories based on fact, including Luton Town Football Club. Many photographs.
THREADS OF TIME: Shela Porter. The life of a remarkable mother and businesswoman, spanning the entire century and based in Hitchin and (mainly) Bedford.
FARM OF MY CHILDHOOD, 1925-1947: Mary Roberts. An almost vanished lifestyle on a remote farm near Flitwick.
STICKS AND STONES: The Life and Times of a Journeyman Printer in Hertford, Dunstable, Cheltenham and Wolverton: Harry Edwards.
CRIME IN HERTFORDSHIRE Volume 1 Law and Disorder: Simon Walker. Authoritative, detailed survey of the changing legal process over many centuries.
JOURNEYS INTO HERTFORDSHIRE: Anthony Mackay. A foreword by The Marquis of Salisbury, Hatfield House. Introducing nearly 200 superbly detailed line drawings.
LEAFING THROUGH LITERATURE: Writers' Lives in Herts and Beds: David Carroll. Illustrated short biographies of many famous authors and their connections with these counties.
A PILGRIMAGE IN HERTFORDSHIRE: H.M. Alderman. Classic, between-the-wars tour round the county, embellished with line drawings.
THE VALE OF THE NIGHTINGALE: Molly Andrews. Several generations of a family, lived against a Harpenden backdrop.
SUGAR MICE AND STICKLEBACKS: Childhood Memories of a Hertfordshire Lad: HarryEdwards.Vivid evocation of gentle pre-war in an archetypal village, Hertingfordbury.
SWANS IN MY KITCHEN: Lis Dorer. Story of a Swan Sanctuary near Hemel Hempstead.
MYSTERIOUS RUINS: The Story of Sopwell, St.Albans: Donald Pelletier. Still one of the town's most atmospheric sites. Sopwell's history is full of fluctuations and interest, mainly as a nunnery associated with St.Albans Abbey.
THE HILL OF THE MARTYR: An Architectural History of St.Albans Abbey: Eileen Roberts. Scholarly and readable chronological narrative history of Hertfordshire and Bedfordshire's famous cathedral. Fully illustrated with photographs and plans.
THE TALL HITCHIN INSPECTOR'S CASEBOOK: A Victorian Crime Novel Based on Fact: Edgar Newman. Worthies of the time encounter more archetypal villains.

SPECIALLY FOR CHILDREN

VILLA BELOW THE KNOLLS: A Story of Roman Britain: Michael Dundrow. An exciting adventure for young John in Totternhoe and Dunstable two thousand years ago.
THE RAVENS: One Boy Against the Might of Rome: James Dyer. On the Barton Hills and in the south-east of England as the men of the great fort of Ravensburgh (near Hexton) confront the invaders.

TITLES ACQUIRED BY THE BOOK CASTLE

BEDFORDSHIRE WILDLIFE: B.S. Nau, C.R. Boon, J.P. Knowles for the Bedfordshire Natural History Society. Over 200 illustrations, maps, photographs and tables survey the plants and animals of this varied habitat.

BIRDS OF BEDFORDSHIRE: Paul Trodd and David Kramer. Environments, breeding maps and details of 267 species, with dozens of photographs, illustrations and diagrams.

A BEDFORDSHIRE QUIZ BOOK: Eric G. Meadows. Wide ranging quizzes and picture puzzles on the history, people, places and bygones of the county.

CURIOSITIES OF BEDFORDSHIRE: A County Guide to the Unusual: Pieter and Rita Boogaart. Quirky, well-illustrated survey of little-known features throughout the county.

THE BIRDS OF HERTFORDSHIRE: Tom Gladwin and Bryan Sage. Essays, maps and records for all 297 species, plus illustrations, photographs and other plates.

BUTTERFLIES OF HERTFORDSHIRE: Brian Sawford. History and ecological guide, with colour photographs and maps for nearly 50 species.

WELWYN RAILWAYS: Tom Gladwin, Peter Neville, Douglas White. A history of the Great Northern line from 1850 to 1986, as epitomised by the five mile stretch between Welwyn Garden City and Woolmer Green. Profusely illustrated in colour and black and white - landscape format.

LIFE AND TIMES OF THE GREAT EASTERN RAILWAY (1839-1922): Harry Paar and Adrian Gray. Personalities, accidents, traffic and tales, plus contemporary photographs and old o.s. maps of this charming railway that transformed East Anglia and Hertfordshire between 1839 and 1922.

THE QUACK: Edgar Newman. Imaginative faction featuring characters in a nineteenth-century painting of a busy Hitchin market scene - especially quack doctor William Mansell.

D-DAY TO ARNHEIM - with Hertfordshire's Gunners: Major Robert Kiln. Vivid, personal accounts of the D-Day preparations and drama, and the subsequent Normandy battles, plus photographs and detailed campaign maps.

THE BOOK CASTLE
12 Church Street, Dunstable
Bedfordshire LU5 4RU
Tel: (01582) 605670 Fax (01582) 662431
Email: bc@book-castle.co.uk
Website: www.book-castle.co.uk

KENILWORTH SUNSET
A Luton Town supporter's journal
by Tim Kingston

About the book: This book is much more than a match record of the 1996/7 Luton Town season. It's funny, it's frank, it's full of the agony and the ecstasy -not forgetting the downright mediocrity -intrinsic in supporting a lower league side.

Oh, but it wasn't always that way. The Hatters' glory days remain fresh in the memory -and many of those memories are woven into this book. Thereby, the match against Crewe in December 1996 is followed by an account of a game at Leicester in 1984 and the debut of a certain Mick Harford. Blackpool at home followed by an away game at Spurs ten years previously -and so on.

A HATTER GOES MAD
by
Kristina Howells

About the book: Highs and lows in the history of Luton Town as told to a young female fan by, amongst others... Mick Harford, Bob Morton, Brian Stein, Trevor Peake, Steve Foster, Paul Walsh, Wally Shanks, Ken Hawkes and David Pleat.

Relive with these names and many others the thrills of promotion, the euphoria of Wembley, the trauma of the Millwall riots, the tension and drama of relegation scraps.

The
Book
Castle

SPECIAL OFFER FOR ALL HATTERS FANS

The Book Castle is offering our 2 previously published football books for the fantastic price of £5.00 the pair.

A Hatter Goes Mad	**Normally retails at £7.99**
Kenilworth Sunset	**Normally retails at £8.99**

ORDER FORM: Special Offer Football Books

To: The Book Castle, 12 Church Street, Dunstable, Beds, LU5 4RU
Tel: 01582 605670

I wish to order.........set/sets at £5.00 the pair (plus £1.60 p & p)

I enclose a cheque for £........... payable to "The Book Castle" OR

Please debit my Visa/Mastercard/Amex card, details as below

Card no ....Expiry Date...................

Signature...

Please post to the address below   (p & p £1.60 extra per order)

Name..

Address...

....

Telephone... Date...

N.B. Offer also available at The Book Castle and selected outlets